A Different Kind of Teacher

*A practical guide to understanding and
resolving difficulties within the school*

TONY HUMPHREYS, BA, HDE, MA, PhD

Newleaf

Newleaf
an imprint of
Gill & Macmillan Ltd
Hume Avenue, Park West
Dublin 12
with associated companies throughout the world
www.gillmacmillan.ie
© Tony Humphreys 1993, 1996
0 7171 2489 4

Index compiled by Helen Litton
Print origination by
Carrigboy Typesetting Services, Co. Cork
Printed in Malaysia

*The paper used in this book is made from the wood pulp of
managed forests. For every tree felled, at least one tree is
planted, thereby renewing natural resources.*

A catalogue record for this book is available from the British Library.

8 10 9 7

Other titles by the author

Self-esteem: The Key to Your Child's Education
The Family: Love It and Leave It
The Power of 'Negative' Thinking

For Helen

Acknowledgments

The people I most want to acknowledge are all the primary and second-level teachers who came to my courses, revealing their needs and challenging my responses to them. I am also indebted to the individual teachers and students who during therapy provided me with insights into school and classroom systems.

A special thanks to Mr Tony Doyle, Director of In-service, in Mary Immaculate College of Education, Limerick, who initiated and organised the courses that I am involved in there on an annual basis.

A special thank you to my partner Helen who was the sounding-board for many of my ideas.

Contents

INTRODUCTION

Recent research in education has revealed that 'how' a teacher teaches is as important as 'what' she teaches. Indeed, the 'how' largely determines effectiveness. It is related to the teacher's level of self-esteem and the ability, or lack of it, to form close relationships with students. The 'how' also involves awareness and practice of positive classroom management approaches. Furthermore, an individual teacher's effectiveness is enhanced by a whole-school management style and by effective leadership within the school system.

The three major sources of stress in teaching are role load, staff relationships and difficult students. Research indicates that the effects of role load are considerably reduced where there is strong staff cohesiveness and cooperation. Also, the teacher who has high self-esteem complains far less of discipline problems than the teacher with middle or poor self-esteem. These observations have been substantiated by findings that the effective school is characterised by high expectations, emotional responsiveness and effective leadership. High expectations mean believing in each student's ability to learn and placing the emphasis on effort rather than performance. Responsiveness involves a democratic caring approach to students with an emphasis on students taking responsibility for themselves.

Following on the research evidence but, principally, on my own personal experiences of teaching in primary, second-level and third-level education, my involvement with teaching staffs over several years and my therapeutic work with teachers and others suffering personal, interpersonal and occupational conflicts, this book focuses on eight main areas:

- stress management
- self-esteem of teachers
- staff relationships and morale
- self-esteem of students
- emotional and behavioural problems of students and staff

- classroom management
- whole-school approach
- effective leadership.

The book is divided into six chapters, each one focusing on a distinct area relevant to the development of more effective teaching.

Chapter 1 discusses the teaching profession, and why and how it has become highly stressed. It looks at the nature of stress, how to identify the signs of stress, and how to cope and develop personally and professionally from it.

Chapter 2 focuses on the teacher with particular emphasis on self-esteem. It identifies three levels of self-esteem and outlines its effects on the teacher herself and on students and colleagues. It introduces the reader to two communication patterns, introjection and projection, which are revelations of self-esteem problems and have serious effects on relationships within the classroom and staffroom. Most of all, this chapter shows how self-esteem can be changed.

Chapter 3 is given over to the staffroom, a source of much stress for many teachers. Staff relationships, effective communication patterns, staff morale, staff affirmation, responding to rigidity in oneself, principals or colleagues, and problem-solving are all discussed.

The focus of Chapter 4 is on the student. This chapter helps teachers to understand the nature of students' emotional, social and behavioural problems within the school and classroom, and how to respond effectively to their manifestation. Particular emphasis is placed on students' self-esteem: how to identify low self-esteem and how to raise it. The effects of students' self-esteem on motivation and learning are also illustrated.

Chapter 5 attends to the classroom. It distinguishes between problems of overcontrol and undercontrol in students, and how the latter cause the greatest disruption in class, even though the former are indicators of a more at-risk pupil. The chapter also outlines behaviours on the part of the teacher that can precipitate problematic responses from students. It outlines essential aspects of effective classroom management, the design and implementation of effective systems of responsibility for students, and the positive use of sanctions. It also deals with responding to the student who is recalcitrant.

Chapter 6 talks about the school and discusses such issues as what factors make for an effective school, a whole-school approach, effective leadership, coping styles within schools, parent–teacher liaison and school ethos. This chapter emphasises the need for shared responsibility and the need for confrontation by teachers of issues within school systems that need to be altered. It also recommends the development of confidential counselling services for teachers and principals.

The emphasis throughout the book is on five issues:

- personal effectiveness
- development of self-esteem-enhancing relationships within the staffroom and classroom
- creation of a greater insight into, understanding of and positive responding to the emotional, behavioural and social problems of students and teachers
- positive approaches to teaching
- shared responsibility.

The aim is always practical. The book includes examples of problematic situations within staffrooms and classrooms and case-studies I have encountered, and offers tried and tested ways of resolving such conflicts. This book is principally developed from the many problems staff groups have presented to me during staff in-service days and our attempts at effective responses to those issues. At the end of each chapter there is a list of the key insights and key actions that will lead to more effective personal, interpersonal and classroom management.

This book is particularly aimed at primary and second-level school teachers but it has relevance to anybody working in the educational system. It is also relevant to policy-makers as it provides insights into the needs of students, teachers, principals, vice-principals, parents, and others within school systems. Parents will also find the book useful since it offers insights on the problems their children may be experiencing in school, and it also apprises them of how to create a positive environment for learning within the home. This book is for students in the education profession at all levels: in basic training and at diploma, graduate and postgraduate levels. It is also of use to lecturers in education.

A good idea is to read the book through so that you get an overall view of the themes and practices recommended. On the other hand, you may like to turn to a chapter or section on issues that currently concern you. Each chapter can stand on its own as it describes specific insights and skills. You can easily dip into particular sections within chapters. The book could also be usefully employed by a staff group or a group of teachers to work through systematically in order to establish greater school effectiveness.

I hope you will find it helpful in resolving many of the difficulties you face within the teaching profession. During my many years of working with staff groups and giving courses to teacher groups, I have witnessed and been impressed, and indeed overawed, by the commitment, dedication and 'need to know more' of teachers.

Finally, references to problems encountered with staff groups and in case-studies have been sufficiently masked so that anonymity is ensured.

CHAPTER 1

The Teaching Profession

❏ *The nature of stress*
❏ *Signs of stress*
❏ *Teacher stress*
❏ *Teacher 'burn-out'*
❏ *Coping with stress*
  - Balanced lifestyle
  - Healthy diet
  - Physical fitness
  - Relaxation
❏ *Key insights*
❏ *Key actions*

❏ *The nature of stress*

Stress is a relatively new word for human problems in living. It has been borrowed from the field of technology and means 'pressure' or 'strain'. The effects of stress on a population's health are very great. It is reckoned that over two-thirds of visits to general practitioners are due to stress-related problems. The six leading causes of death – heart disease, cancer, cirrhosis of the liver, lung ailments, accidental injuries and suicide – are all directly or indirectly caused by stress. The three best-selling drugs are Valium, which is a tranquilliser, Idera, which is for hypertension (blood pressure) and Tagamet, which is for ulcers and other stomach problems.

It is important to distinguish between what I call *necessary* and *emergency* stress. Necessary stress occurs, for example, when you eat and you put your digestive system under stress; when you run or play games and you put your cardiovascular system under stress; or when, in preparing for a lecture, a certain amount of apprehension pushes adrenalin into your system, mobilises your intellectual resources, and increases your concentration and motivation. However, if you overeat or overexercise or overworry so that your stomach is in a knot, your heart racing and you feel pressure in your head, you are now into emergency stress. The word 'emergency' is very accurate because once you go beyond a certain level of stress you are in an emergency state and something needs to be done to return you to a welfare state. So, for example, a typical cause of stress is the daily hassles of rushing and racing, meeting deadlines, attempting to do too many things at once and so on. If you go into many houses at half-past eight in the morning you will understand the stressful effects of daily hassle. People rush, race, choke back food, shout, roar, argue, make mistakes, cannot remember. Their bodies will reveal the pressure they are putting themselves under: tension headaches, stomach 'butterflies', heart palpitations and other signs. The 'emergency' to be responded to is the rushing, racing and worrying by counterbehaviours such as getting up earlier, doing things calmly and thinking positively. If these corrective behaviours are effective, people will return to a welfare state; if not, the true causes of the emergency stress have not yet been isolated and further analysis is needed.

Certainly a wise course of action for everybody is to learn to live in the present moment. Few people do. Since beginning this book how many times has your mind wandered into the past or out into the future? The skill of present-moment living is to focus totally on the action of the moment, whether it is reading a particular word, peeling a potato or listening to someone. Some readers will no doubt say you have to think about the future and past. Planning for the future is, indeed, important but then planning is a present-moment activity. Worrying about what is going to happen is a future activity and totally redundant. Practising simple time-management will help you plan your day, week, month, or year ahead. It ensures allocation of time for all your essential needs, and the more you meet your different needs the less you are stressed. Likewise, it is important to learn from the past but not to live in it as many people do by regretting, bemoaning, complaining and comparing. Evaluation is a present-moment activity of bringing the benefit of experience to bear in the present.

❏ *Signs of stress*

It is not too difficult to determine your level of stress. Below is a list of the main signs of stress. Go carefully through them and list any symptom you experience. Ask yourself how frequently, for how long and to what degree of intensity (hardly noticeable to very debilitating) you experience the listed symptoms.

Signs of stress	
Emotional signs	• Anxiety • aggression • apathy • boredom • depression • fatigue • frustration • guilt and shame • irritability and bad temper • moodiness • low self-esteem • threat and tension • nervousness • loneliness • hypersensitivity to criticism
Behavioural signs	• Accident proneness • drug taking • temper outbursts • excessive eating or loss of appetite • excessive drinking or smoking • excitability • impulsive behaviour • impaired speech • nervous laughter • restlessness • trembling • rushing • doing too many things at the one time
Cognitive signs	• Inability to make decisions and concentrate • frequent forgetfulness • negative thinking • mental blocks • living in the past or future
Body effects	• Increased heart rate and blood pressure • dryness of mouth • sweating • dilation of pupils • difficulty in breathing • hot and cold spells • a 'lump in the throat' • numbness or tingling in parts of the limbs • stomach butterflies
Health effects	• Asthma • amenorrhoea • chest and back pains • coronary heart disease • diarrhoea • faintness and dizziness • dyspepsia • frequent urination • headaches and ➞

	migraine • neuroses • nightmares • insomnia • psychoses • psychosomatic disorders • diabetes mellitus • skin rash • ulcers • loss of sexual interest • weakness
School effects	• Absenteeism • poor staff relations • poor motivation • high staff turnover rates • poor staff morale • antagonism at work • job dissatisfaction

If you did not list any of the symptoms please consult a clinical psychologist or psychotherapist immediately as you are in massive 'denial'. There is no one without some degree of emergency stress! If you listed most of the signs you should likewise seek help immediately.

Be wary of jumping to conclusions when you experience any of these symptoms. People tend to think the worst so that a persistent headache becomes a sign of a brain tumour, a pain in the chest becomes a sure indicator of heart disease and a discomfiture in the stomach becomes a cancer. Unfortunately such an alarmist response shoots your stress levels up higher so that the symptoms increase in intensity, which in turn convinces you of your catastrophic diagnosis, and the spiralling of panic continues. It reminds me of a teacher who came up to me at the end of a lecture and told me he had been experiencing three of the symptoms on the stress signs checklist for five years. The three symptoms were dryness of the mouth, lower back pain and frequent urination. He had been to a number of medical consultants over the years but no one could explain why he had the symptoms. Nevertheless, he was prescribed painkillers for his back, a spray for his mouth but nothing for the frequent urination. Despite the medical treatment the symptoms had not abated over the years; indeed, at times, they severely escalated. It is always wise to get yourself physically checked out, particularly for some persistent physical symptom. However, if you get a clear bill of physical health, you need to look at possible psychological and social causes of the symptoms. This particular teacher did not;

instead he convinced himself that he had cancer and believed the doctors either were not telling him or had not discovered it. To go around believing you have cancer is extremely frightening and highly stressful and it was no wonder the stress symptoms had not abated.

What often triggers stress is change. I asked the teacher had something changed in his life five years before – did someone close to him die, did he get married, were there marital problems, a new addition to the family, in-laws coming to live-in, loss of status? It was really quite simple; five years before he had taken over the principalship of a large secondary school. It was then the symptoms became apparent. He was very dependent on others for acceptance and approval, had a dread of failure and generally was a worrier. He would always have had a certain level of stress owing to these underlying vulnerabilities. The extra responsibilities heightened the risk of failure and disapproval, and his underlying fears now became heightened and more apparent. The man's problem was certainly not cancer, nor was it lower back pain, dryness of the mouth or frequent urination; neither was it the change to school principalship but rather his long-term vulnerabilities of fears, dependency and low self-esteem. When these were corrected the symptoms which had so scared him disappeared.

Bear in mind that emergency stress is positive! It alerts you to change that is needed in some area of your life. It may be within yourself (self-esteem); it may be interpersonal indicating the need for change in some important relationship; or it may be professional indicating the need for change within some aspect of your work or, in some cases, a total career change. The possibilities are endless. Each person has to find the source of his own stress. If necessity is the mother of invention then stress can be the father of self-actualisation.

❏ *Teacher stress*

Stress in teaching has been getting a fair degree of press in recent years. The number of people wanting to get out of the profession is high and the number going into it is falling. The rise in early retirement on health grounds is unprecedented. What has happened to bring about these changes?

Occupational stress is a function of two main factors: demands and control. When demands in an occupation are high and control is low you have a high-stress job. A low-stress position is the opposite: demands are low and control is high. Air traffic controllers have high-stress work because demands on them are very high as the least mistake may cause a major disaster and control is minimal as air space is taken up very quickly, particularly in the world's busy airports. Librarians, on the other hand, have low demands made on them and they have high control over the rate at which they work. There has been a double shift in these factors within the teaching profession. Within the last two decades the role demands on teachers have increased enormously and control (discipline) issues have become a major problem for many schools. The combination of increased demands and control difficulties has turned teaching into a high-stress occupation. There are differences between schools but all schools will have experienced some increase in stress levels.

A research study carried out in the mid-western area of Ireland distinguished between advantaged (middle-class) schools and disadvantaged (more lower/working-class) schools. The study surveyed the prevalence of educational, behavioural and emotional problems among primary-school children. In the advantaged schools at least 10 per cent of children had serious behavioural and emotional difficulties; in the disadvantaged areas the percentage was considerably higher at 27 per cent. Little or no psychological or social back-up services were available to these schools and teachers, who, though not trained to understand or cope with these difficulties, were nonetheless expected to do so. Such children present many control difficulties within the classroom and, not surprisingly, one of the major causes of teacher stress is students with emotional and behavioural problems. Inadequate classroom and whole-school management systems or resortment to old destructive authoritarian methods serves only to increase control difficulties. Ineffective leadership is another major contributor to stress in teaching as many principals, who may have been effective as teachers, do not lead well. The skills of teaching are very different to the skills of leadership and it is not a Department of Education policy that principals be required to do management courses. Lack of cohesiveness between leaders and staff makes for inconsistency and unpredictability in the management of classrooms and the school. Consistency and predictability are the hallmarks of good management systems and their absence means many control difficulties.

If control problems are increasing in schools so also are the demands made on teachers. These demands principally come from an educational system that has put the emphasis on performance in examinations as the main criterion for successful teaching. The competition for 'points' to get into a third-level college has pressurised second-level educators into an educational philosophy that is discriminatory (students who are considered bright are more reinforced) and conditional (learning not for learning's sake but for points' sake). This is immensely taxing on teachers themselves as they tend to measure their professional effectiveness by examination results. What is even more worrying is that primary schools now view entrance examinations to secondary schools as a major goal, for which preparations begin in fifth class. There is also an increase in interschool competition measured by how many children get into the 'best' schools.

Examinations measure only an aspect of academic development. To evaluate teaching on such a narrow criterion would do serious injustice to teachers who help poorly motivated children to develop from low levels of learning to moderate levels of learning. It is little credit to teachers to bring highly motivated students to high examination results. Yet the emphasis and appraisal tend to be on these students. Furthermore, education is not just about academic development. Surely of equal importance is the emotional, social, sexual, physical, behavioural, spiritual and creative development of children? Indeed, educational research is now showing that the emotional development of children in the classroom and school is of primary importance. Children with learning difficulties generally have low self-esteem and unless their emotional problems are corrected remedial efforts tend to have minimal effects. Marital breakdown, unemployment, profound social and political changes, the fall in religious practice – all serve to make more demands on teachers. Bureaucracy and its obsessive need for paperwork makes for more demands, particularly on principals and vice-principals, who very often do not have any secretarial assistance. Many principals are also under pressure because of demoralisation among their teaching staff. Finally, the fact that the profession is not a well-paid one and that promotion is limited does not help matters.

❑ *Teacher 'burn-out'*

The effects of occupational stress have become known as 'burn-out'. The main signs of burn-out are listed below. Again, in checking through this list, evaluate the frequency, intensity and duration of the symptoms you have experienced.

Main signs of burn-out	
• Absenteeism • Physical exhaustion • Appetite problems (under- or overeating) • Insomnia • Psychosomatic complaints, e.g. headaches, back pain, chest pain, stomach problems, bowel problems • Irritability • Reliance on drugs such as alcohol, tranquillisers, antidepressants, nicotine	• Pessimism and fatalism • Increasing discouragement • Negative attitudes to teaching and to students • Poor relationships with colleagues • Loss of self-esteem • Loss of motivation to develop oneself • Reduced involvement in life • Loss of creativity

Occupational burn-out is rarely a product purely of the job itself. Generally, a combination of personal vulnerability and occupational stress brings about burn-out. A case history will illustrate this point. This was a teacher who had been teaching for fifteen years. In the year prior to coming to see me she had an extremely difficult leaving certificate examination class. This teacher was very dependent on academic results as a measure of her worth as a person, and this dependency made her hypersensitive to any criticism or disapproval; certainly, failure in terms of poor academic results highly threatened her self-esteem. Consequently, she worked tooth and nail to bring this class up to 'her standards'. She was under constant strain during the year. At the end of the academic year she was emotionally drained and physically exhausted. But, rather than sighing with relief that the year was over and she could enjoy the three best things about teaching, June, July and August, she now worried about what the examination results would reveal. When the results came out in August the 'difficult' class did quite well and now rather than clapping herself on the back for a job well done, she worried and fretted that if she got another class like that in September she would not be able to cope. By the time September came she had immobilised herself with fear and was unable to return to school. When she came to see me in mid-October absenteeism was total – she had not returned to school at all. There were dark circles under her eyes revealing physical exhaustion, insomnia and loss of appetite. She was on both antidepressants and tranquillisers. She complained of severe headaches and nausea. She felt she could no longer cope with teaching and students. Her discouragement was total and her loss of self-esteem was serious as she now saw herself as 'a total failure'. She was pessimistic and fatalistic about the future, and her motivation and involvement in life had plummeted. She sat around most of the time brooding about her problems, which served only to increase them.

This description is typical of many teachers I have helped over the years. Her burn-out resulted from the combination of her own poor self-esteem with accompanying dependency and multiple fears *and* the increased pressure from the difficult examination class. The help that is needed in such cases is personal empowerment to elevate self-esteem and independence of others and of performance; more constructive approaches to teaching; and, whenever possible, the development of a supportive and dynamic staffroom environment. When at least some of these issues are resolved the stressed teacher is able to return to work.

❏ *Coping with stress*

As has been seen stress is positive as it indicates the need for change. Furthermore, each person has to detect the source of his own stress and on discovery take corrective action. Nevertheless, there are coping actions that help all people under stress even though they rarely resolve the underlying issue unique to each person's stress problems. Stress management clinics have mushroomed all over America and they are beginning to appear in Ireland. These clinics tend to focus on four main coping skills:

- balanced lifestyle
- healthy diet
- physical exercise
- relaxation.

■ Balanced lifestyle

Many people referred with stress-related diseases like heart disease, ulcers, back pain, etc. typically present with imbalanced lifestyles. I remember many years ago lecturing to a group of medical doctors on the wonders of clinical hypnosis. At the end of the presentation I sat down to take questions and my lower back went into spasm. The pain was excruciating and through clenched teeth I cancelled the questions session. How embarrassing! There was I heralding the wonders of clinical hypnosis and then I collapsed with psychosomatic pain. The medical doctors wanted to cart me off to hospital. However, I knew what the problem was. I persuaded them to get me down on to the carpeted floor and inject the muscle concerned with a muscle relaxant. Unfortunately, the spasm had gone too far and could not be controlled. Eventually, I had them slide me into the back seat of my car, drive me to my home and put me to bed. I knew the only answer was bed rest. Here was a loud 'emergency' signal for me. Indeed, I had been getting twinges of pain for some time but had ignored them. When a symptom is ignored it has to get louder in order to alert the person to the stress being created and the changes that are needed. The apparent cause of the lower back pain was overwork. At the time I was working between seventy and eighty hours weekly between therapy and lecturing. I took the advice of developing a more balanced lifestyle and began to time-manage all my major personal, interpersonal and professional needs. I also resurrected my ability to self-hypnotise and to breathe diaphragmatically. I delegated more work to colleagues, took up tennis and walking to strengthen my body, took much more care of my diet and planned regular holidays. All in all it was a commendable effort to reduce my stress levels.

Did it work? For six months I maintained the effort and I had no reoccurrence of the severe pain. However, after six months I found myself increasing my workload. Clearly, I had not got to the bottom of my compulsion to overwork. A question I would have needed to ask myself six months previously was 'why am I overworking?' Certainly the imbalanced lifestyle due to the long working hours was the surface reason for my emergency stress level but a much deeper reason had yet to be dealt with and failure to deal with it explained the gradual return to old neglectful ways. The answer to the question was an inability to say 'no' to people who needed help or made requests of me. This non-assertiveness was due to my identity being tied up with being the helper. When I was a child my mother was wheelchair-bound and it was I who mostly looked after her and the other members of the family. Relatives and others used to say 'what a marvellous child' who can cook, shop, clean the house and take care of his mother. To say 'no' would subconsciously mean losing this regard and becoming invisible in the eyes of others. Such is the effect of a conditional upbringing.

Now I can say 'no', not all of the time, but much of the time. I have learned that my identity is separate from what I do and that my needs deserve as much consideration as do the needs of others. Inevitably, people with self-esteem problems are neglectful of many of their essential needs. It requires considerable discipline to correct this imbalance and the best approach is through simple time-management so that you ensure that at least most of your essential needs are met within any one couple of days. We have many different need areas in our lives and each one needs to be responded to. So check the following list and see how well and how often you meet your needs:

Checklist of needs
• Emotional needs of love, affection, warmth, closeness, support, understanding, compassion, challenge, humour.
• Cognitive needs of intellectual stimulation, reading, discussion, challenge, problem-solving, responsibility.
• Behavioural needs for the development of a whole range of skills – cooking, painting, dressing, writing, car maintenance, gardening, woodwork.
• Social needs for friendship, companionship, sharing of expertise and knowledge.
• Physical needs for health, fitness, comfort, safety, food and warmth.
• Sensual needs so that the five senses receive adequate stimulation.
• Occupational needs for meaningful work, fair salary, good conditions, recognition for input, staff cohesiveness and support, benefit systems, promotional opportunities.
• Sexual needs for gratification of sexual drive within the context of a mature and loving relationship.
• Recreational needs for rest, games, sports, hobbies, interests.
• Spiritual needs for transcendence, mystical experiences and meaningful explanation for existence.

Remember if you fail to keep to a balanced lifestyle then there is some deeper issue that needs to be detected and a deeper level of responding is required.

■ Healthy diet

Your energy is maintained by three main sources: sleep, food and fitness. To be beneficial food needs to be nourishing. Also, it is important that your diet follows your energy pattern. Many books on diet suggest that breakfast is the most important meal of the day, but my body does not agree with that suggestion. Following a night's sleep my energy level is high and I do not feel particularly hungry. I am a great believer in listening to what my body says, so in the morning I tend to have a light breakfast of fresh orange juice, two slices of brown bread and a cup of coffee. However, come lunchtime, after working some four or five hours, my body sends messages of starvation and I tend to eat my main meal of the day then. If I do not respond to my low energy levels, expressed through hunger, I find by mid-afternoon I am drowsy and headachy. However, when I eat a good wholesome meal I find I can continue to work up to 7.00 p.m. without any symptoms of fatigue. By that time I am hungry once more, and I will eat again but not a big meal as at lunchtime. It is unfortunate that many professionals have made lunch what I call 'a banana and yoghurt affair' and that their main meal is eaten in the evening when not as much energy is needed to complete the day's activities.

Junk foods which have no energy value should be avoided. Most packaged foods have taken the good out of food; regrettably, most 'convenience' food is packaged. It is best to avoid packaged food and eat as much fresh foods as possible. One further issue is not to use food as a substitute for other needs like love, comfort, warmth and support or not to use food as a means of reducing fear. Both of these responses to unmet needs only create another problem which is overeating and obesity.

■ Physical fitness

People who are physically fit withstand the physiological effects of stress better than those who are physically unfit. Common sense, you may say, but it always puzzles me why good sense is called common sense as it tends to be a very rare commodity indeed! 'Rare sense' would be a more accurate term. It does not take too much to establish physical fitness but what it does take is regularity. Thirty to forty minutes, four or five times weekly, of a moderate-type exercise like walking, swimming, tennis or cycling is all that is required. Weekend athleticism is of little or no use. Furthermore, be sure you perspire when you exercise, otherwise you may only be 'dawdling' which is not physical exercise of a worthwhile nature. Do not exercise beyond tiredness or exhaustion as this overstresses your body and, if done regularly, puts you at risk. Many keep-fit fanatics suffer early disease or death as excessive exercising is an abuse of your physical system and eventually leads to physical breakdown. If in reading this you have been thinking 'where am I going to find thirty to forty minutes, four or five times weekly?', please return to the section on balanced lifestyle. Routine helps in the establishment of an exercise regime. But be flexible in your routine, as rigid adherence to any behaviour has its own inbuilt stressor.

▪ Relaxation

There is evidence that regular practice of relaxation can add considerably to one's life-span. Relaxation, to my mind, is an essential requisite for all teachers. One of my recommendations to teachers is that, no matter how disruptive, aggressive or uncooperative students are, stay totally calm and unflappable. It is important that students perceive that their irresponsible behaviour has no control over you. If you lose your cool in the face of their problematic behaviours they will be quick to spot this weakness and exploit it for their own needs. Furthermore, a teacher needs at all times to model self-control; by staying relaxed and calm but firm, you exhibit the control you expect of students in the classroom and school corridors. However, if in teaching you shout and roar to gain control of a class, students are quick to see the hypocrisy of this demand and may not respond to your negative overtures for responsibility on their part. There is a far greater likelihood that matters will de-escalate if the teacher remains calm and relaxed.

Relaxation is a skill that needs practice, just like driving a car, playing golf and playing the piano. However, relaxation is not resting. Curled up in front of a glowing fire, with a brandy and the Late Late Show on TV, is resting but not relaxation. Relaxation is a deeper experience and stretches from light and medium to deep and trance levels. At the beginning of training yourself to relax it is good to practise an exercise twice daily for ten to fifteen minutes at a time. I have included a five-minute exercise and a tension-releasing exercise below but I would recommend attending relaxation classes for a more in-depth understanding and experience of relaxation. The aim is to be able eventually to bring the relaxation response into all life situations, and particularly stressful situations like conflict incidences within classrooms or staffrooms. There are many types of relaxation methods, for example yoga, transcendental meditation, progressive muscular relaxation, hypnosis, autogenics and visualisation. Different methods suit different people: if you have a vivid imagination you could use visualisation methods; if you are more interested in physical activity, then muscular relaxation or yoga might suit; and if you have retained trance ability from childhood then hypnotic approaches would be appropriate. Relaxation is a lifelong skill that everyone needs to develop, but most of all adults who have the charge of the mature development of children.

These four coping mechanisms – balanced lifestyle, healthy diet, physical exercise and relaxation – are a good starting-point in establishing a positive lifestyle. When they become a routine part of your behaviour you are in a better position to begin to explore deeper levels of change that may be needed in your personal, interpersonal and professional life.

Relaxation exercises

Quick release of tension exercise

Whenever you feel anxious, panicky or uptight . . .

1 Let your breath go (don't breathe in first).
2 Take in a slow, gentle breath; hold it for a second.
3 Let it go, with a leisurely sigh of relief.
4 Drop your shoulders at the same time and relax your hands.
5 Make sure your teeth are not clenched together.
6 If you have to speak, speak more slowly and in a lower tone of voice.

....

Short relaxation exercise

This exercise is designed for when you have only a short time to spare. It is better to have a chair with arms but ideally you should be able to relax anywhere you find yourself. Use a cushion in the small of the back if it helps. Make sure you are warm.

➡

Sit upright and well back in the chair so that your thighs and back are supported; rest your hands in the cradle position on your lap or lightly on top of your thighs. If you like, take off your shoes, and let your feet rest on the ground (if they don't touch the floor, try to find a book or similar object to rest them on). If you want to, close your eyes.

Begin by breathing out first. Then breathe in easily, just as much as you need. Now breathe out slowly, with a slight sigh, like a balloon slowly deflating. Do this once more, slowly . . . breathe in . . . breathe out . . . as you breathe out, feel the tension begin to drain away. Then go back to your ordinary breathing, even, quiet, steady.

Now direct your thoughts to each part of your body in turn, to the muscles and joints.

Think first about your left foot. Your toes are still. Your foot feels heavy on the floor. Let your foot and toes start to feel completely relaxed.

Now think about your right foot . . . toes . . . ankle . . . they are resting heavily on the floor. Let both your feet, your toes and ankles start to relax.

Now think about your legs. Let your legs feel completely relaxed and heavy on the chair. Your thighs, your knees roll outwards when they relax, so let them go.

Think now about your back and your spine. Let the tension drain away from your back, and from your spine. Follow your breathing, and each time you breathe out, relax your back and spine a little more.

Let your abdominal muscles become soft and loose. There's no need to hold your stomach in tight, it rises and falls as you breathe quietly. Feel that your stomach is completely relaxed.

No tension in your chest. Let your breathing be slow and easy, and each time you breathe out, let it go a little more.

Think now about the fingers of your left hand . . . they are curved, limp and quite still. Now the fingers of your right hand . . . relaxed . . . soft and still. Let this feeling of relaxation spread . . . up your arms . . . feel the heaviness in your arms . . . up to your shoulders. Let your shoulders relax, let them drop easily . . . and then let them drop even further than you thought they could. Think about your neck. Feel the tension melt away from your neck and shoulders. Each time you breathe out, relax your neck a little more.

Before we move on, just check to see if all these parts of your body are still relaxed – your feet, legs, back and spine, stomach, hands, arms, neck and shoulders. Keep your breathing gentle and easy. Every time you breathe out, relax a little more and let all the tension ease away from your body. No tension – just enjoy this feeling of relaxation.

Now think about your face. Let the expression come off your face. Smooth out your brow, and let your forehead feel wide and relaxed. Let your eyebrows drop gently. There is no tension around your eyes, your eyelids slightly closed, your eyes are still. Let your jaw unwind, teeth slightly apart as your jaw unwinds more and more. Feel the relief of letting go.

Now think about your tongue and throat. Let your tongue drop down to the bottom of your mouth and relax completely. Relax your tongue and throat. And your lips slightly parted, no pressure between them. Let all the muscles in your face unwind and let go . . . there is no tension in your face . . . just let it relax more and more.

Now, instead of thinking about yourself in parts, feel the all-over sensation of letting go, of quiet and of rest. Check to see if you are still relaxed. Stay like this for a few moments, and listen to your breathing . . . in . . . and out . . . let your body become looser, heavier, each time you breathe out.

Continue for a little longer, and enjoy this time for relaxation.

Coming back – slowly, move your hands a little and your feet. When you are ready, open your eyes and sit quiet for a while. Stretch, if you want to, or yawn, and slowly start to move again.

❑ *Key insights*

- There is a distinction to be made between 'necessary' and 'emergency' stress.
- A life-event often triggers a stress response.
- Stress is positive; it alerts one to the need for change.
- Occupational stress is a function of high demands and low control.
- Multiple role demands, students with behavioural and emotional problems, staff relationships and ineffective leadership are the main sources of stress in teaching.

- Education is not just about academic development but also involves responding to the emotional, social, sexual, spiritual, behavioural and physical needs of each student.
- Low self-esteem of students is the main contributor to poor academic functioning.
- Burn-out in teachers arises from a combination of personal vulnerability and occupational stress.

❑ *Key actions*

- Live in the present moment.
- Detect your own stress symptoms.
- Identify your own unique sources of stress.
- Be wary of 'denial' of stress experiences.
- Holistically evaluate a recurrent symptom – do not jump to the 'worst' conclusion.
- Practise these coping mechanisms: balanced lifestyle, healthy diet, physical fitness and relaxation.
- Keep calm and unflappable in the face of problematic behaviours in the classroom and staffroom.

The Teacher

❏ *Importance of self-esteem*

There are many personal and professional reasons why teachers need to look at the whole area of self-worth. Medical evidence shows a strong correlation between physical health and longevity and high self-esteem. Likewise psychiatry and psychology have shown that people's problems in living are related to personal vulnerability and feelings of inferiority. Family and marital well-being are strongly related to the high self-esteem of parents and partners. Indeed, the well-being of all human systems is determined by the level of self-esteem of its participants. Clearly, leaders have a high responsibility to increase their self-esteem as problematic self-esteem on their behalf leads to ineffective leadership. Finally, the teacher with high self-esteem produces students with high self-esteem and, sadly, the converse is also true.

What is self-esteem? Basically self-esteem has to do with how you feel about two aspects of yourself – lovability and capability. Many of the clients I work with state that they see nothing about themselves that is lovable, and neither do they see themselves as being capable of doing anything. The perception is often totally contrary to the obvious beauty, attractiveness, creativity, high intelligence and ability of the person. Dorothy Corkille Briggs sums it up very well in a book entitled *Your Child's Self-Esteem*: 'A person's judgement of self influences the kind of friends he chooses, how he gets along with others, the kind of person he marries and how productive he will be. It affects his creativity, integrity, stability and even whether he will be a leader or a follower. His feeling of self-worth forms the core of his personality and determines the uses he makes of his aptitudes and abilities. His attitude toward himself has a direct bearing on how he lives all parts of his life. In fact, self-esteem is the mainspring that slates each of us for success or failure as a human being'.

❑ *Levels of self-esteem*

Each person who reads this book has a particular level of self-worth, which can be usefully categorised as high, middle or low self-esteem.

Indicators of high self-esteem	
• Independent	• Acceptance of self and others
• Open and spontaneous	• Respects and values others' differences
• Optimistic, excited and challenged by life	• Listens to others
• Flexible	• Can take criticism and feedback
• Direct and clear communicator	• Tolerant of frustration
• Owns own problems, feelings, perceptions, ambitions etc.	• Physically healthy
	• Emotionally mature
• Emotional closeness with a few significant others	• Encouraging of self and others
	• Realistic awareness of strengths and weaknesses ➜

• Sees weaknesses as opportunities for developing strength • Problem-solver • Expressive of all feelings • Resistant to conformity • Seeks support, advice, help, comfort when needed • Wholehearted involvement in all aspects of life	• Trusts and values self • Caring of others • Positively firm with self and others who attempt to impose artificial values • Cares for environment • Spiritual • Needs privacy

Indicators of middle self-esteem	
• Dependent • Approval-seeker • People-pleaser • Difficulties in seeking support, help, advice etc. • Cautious and unadventurous • Fearful of new situations • Can take some criticism • Moderate degree of optimism • Critical of others' differences • Threatened by opposition • Expressive of some feelings • Conformist • Doubts about various aspects of self: physical, intellectual, social, etc. • Unsure • General feeling of dissatisfaction • Blaming of others	• Denial of problems • Insecure in relationships • Compares oneself to others • Jealous of others' success, possessions etc. • Critical of self and others • Some neglect of physical welfare • Aggressive or passive • Intolerant of frustration • Compliant or rigid • Lives in the future • Low autonomy • Very ambitious • Hostile sense of humour • Perfectionist • Tendencies to worry and anxiety

Indicators of low self-esteem	
• Highly dependent • Pessimistic and fatalistic • No sense of 'good' about self • Condemning of self • Extreme perfectionism • 'Drop-out' • Extreme fear of new situations • Highly critical of all aspects of self • Believes everybody else is better off • Deep inferiority complex or superiority complex (which is a cover-up of a sense of inferiority) • Lonely and isolated • Inability to form close and deep emotional relation-ships • Sees oneself as unlovable • Sometimes suicidal • Rigid and inflexible • Highly blaming of others or total denial of vulnerabilities • Bottles up feelings or can be dangerously aggressive and violent • Neglectful of physical welfare • Rejecting of self • Possessive of others • Constant need for reassurance • Manipulative of others	• Feelings easily hurt • Highly sensitive to criticism • Engages in protective communication (for example, hostile silences, sulking, sarcasm, cynicism, blaming, ridiculing) • Resistant to change • Cannot take compliments or positive feedback • Continually unhappy • Troubled relationships with others • Worrier • Highly prone to anxiety and depression • Moody • Feels different from all others • Guilty about pleasure experiences for self • Fears rejection • Fearful of mistakes and failure • Indecisive • Lives life according to 'shoulds', 'should nots', 'have tos', 'musts' and 'ought tos' • Ashamed of self • Feels life is not worth living • Overinvolvement or under-involvement in other people's lives • Constantly trying to prove self

A teacher's level of self-esteem determines her level of professional esteem: high self-esteem leads to being an effective teacher and middle to low self-esteem leads to levels of ineffectiveness.

❏ *Origins of self-esteem*

The causes of self-esteem lie principally in the early experiences of childhood. These early relationships with the significant adults in our lives (parents, relatives, teachers) were generally of a mixed nature in terms of being positive and negative. The positive interactions formed an image of being lovable and capable, whilst the negative ones developed a sense of unlovability and incapability. Clearly, the emphasis which obtained determines the level of self-esteem. Parents, teachers, and others are mirrors for children: the child who mostly experiences physical and emotional affection, affirmation, praise, encouragement, support, tenderness, listening, challenge, play and positive firmness forms a healthy self-image, whilst the child who frequently experiences absence of affection or caring that is unfeeling, ridiculing, scolding, critical and physically abusive, or who endures hostile silences, unrealistic demands and standards, and negative labelling develops an inferior image of self. No child has only positive experiences and as a result there are very few people with high self-esteem. Most people have middle self-esteem and a sizeable number have low levels.

One of the major sources of neuroses in our society, and one which few escape being influenced by, is conditionality. A conditional upbringing breeds anxiety, uncertainty and insecurity, and its intensity determines levels of anxiety and dependency. Conditional valuing means that one is loved, not for one's person or being, but for one's behaviour. Love then becomes a weapon to be used when children do not measure up to behavioural expectations. It reminds me of a young mother whose parents had both been teachers and who were highly demanding in terms of 'being perfect'. This young woman had a young child of less than two years in age who was always perfectly dressed. Inevitably, one day the child messed her perfect little suit. Her mother lost control and began to shout at the child: 'Mother doesn't love you anymore, she doesn't love you, she doesn't love you' – and she kept at it and at it. The child went very quiet and was as 'good as gold' for the rest of the day. An hour after the child was put to bed that night there were cries and roars from her room. Her mother ran upstairs to find the child standing up in her cot convulsed with crying. On seeing her mother the child immediately blubbered: 'Mummy, Mummy, do you love me?' The child clearly had had a nightmare awakening her to the unresolved trauma of that day. How clever of the child's psyche! The message to the mother was: 'If you keep withdrawing love from me because of my behaviour my life will become a nightmare'. Children's nightmares are often messages to parents, teachers and other adults about conflicts inside the children regarding relationships with adults.

Conditions for love operate within most family and educational systems. Typical conditions are:

• Be good	• Be pretty
• Be perfect	• Be handsome
• Be like me	• Be Irish
• Be quiet	• Be Unionist
• Be clever	• Be Catholic
• Be successful	• Be busy
• Be kind	• Be like your brother/sister
• Be funny	

In the classroom it is known that teachers make more eye contact with, lean towards and ask more questions of children whom they consider 'bright pupils'. Every child, indeed every adult, needs to shout from the rooftops, 'I am not my behaviour'. Relationships are broken time and time again over bits of behaviour. It is important to let others know what behaviours please and displease but only within the context of an enduring valuing relationship. The most common phobia of all is the fear of public speaking. A clear condition that was imposed on nearly everybody in childhood was 'do not make a fool of yourself' and hence public speaking becomes a threat to self-esteem. To take another example of conditionality, research indicates that the children of teachers tend to be more

psychologically at risk than the children of any other professional group. The condition operating would seem to be: 'As a
teacher, how could I have a fool of a child!'

Cutting the ties that bind us and the conditions that
enchain us is one of the primary tasks of building self-esteem.
Conditionality breeds all sorts of dependencies – on success,
acceptance, approval, performance, physical appearance. The
reverse side of the conditional coin is fear – of failure, rejection, criticism, loss of prestige, loss of physical looks. Fear in
its turn creates negative, pessimistic, fatalistic and tentative
attitudes and thoughts to life and leads to behaviours that either
are of an avoidant, shy, withdrawing or hidden nature, or are
aggressive, overbearing, intense or blaming in style. The combination and intensity of all these emotions, attitudes and
behaviours can have a profound effect on physical health.

❏ *Self-esteem and teaching*

In the classroom the teacher with middle to low self-esteem
tends to be defensive, sensitive to criticism and intolerant of
difference from her viewpoint, and to personalise students'
inappropriate behaviours as messages about her performance
as a teacher rather than as revelations of the students' inner
conflicts. Staying separate from students' irresponsible behaviour is a key issue for teachers. However, vulnerability to
criticism blinds a teacher to this reality and unless this vulnerability is resolved it is difficult to stay separate. The
vulnerable teacher also projects her own dependencies onto
students, particularly those involving performance and success.
Personalisation occurs when a teacher confuses a student's
troublesome behaviours with her own identity whereas with
projection the teacher confuses her own behaviour with the
student's identity.

An example of personalisation or introjection comes from
the case of a fourteen-year-old student who was sent to me
because he had been suspended from school. The suspension
was a sanction for writing in the class workbook: 'Fuck you
teacher'. On reading it the teacher reacted in a personalised
way and complained to her principal that 'nobody treats me
like that' – the boy was duly suspended. Certainly the boy's

written aggression was unacceptable but it was a statement, albeit hidden, about the boy not about the teacher. The boy needed to be educated to communicate in a more appropriate way. The hidden issue, which neither principal nor class teacher had looked for, was that the class teacher had embarrassed the boy in front of his peers and on sitting down after the experience, feeling hugely angry, he wrote his aggressive statement. He then forgot about it, and later on in the day handed up his workbook for evaluation. Both teacher and student could have learned much from this incident. A teacher does not have the right to embarrass students in front of their peers. Sarcasm, cynicism, ridicule and scoldings are unfair weapons to be used in classrooms. The use of them triggers defences against threats to self-esteem, such as aggressive behaviour. This class teacher could have benefited from becoming aware of her unproductive action and also from apologising to the boy with a determination not to hurt him again. The boy, in his turn, could have been taught how to communicate his grievance clearly, directly and discreetly to the teacher, and made aware that any form of aggression is unacceptable and deserves some sanction. Such an outcome also would have strengthened the relationship between the student and the teacher.

Projection is present in the person who attempts to establish her worth through the behaviour or person of another. So, for example, a teacher who is dependent on others for approval may put undue pressure on her students to perform academically so that she can gain approval from colleagues, parents and students themselves. It is now well established that suicide increases around examination times, especially leaving certificate and first university examinations. The suicidal student, feeling unable to meet the expectations (projections) of parents, will commit suicide rather than face the humiliation of failure and the consequent rejection by parents.

A classic illustration of the devastating effects of projection (people living their lives through their children or students) was a case of two brothers I helped when I was practising in England. Both boys were taught by both of their parents in primary school (rarely a good idea). The projection from both parents was that their sons should be top of the class. There was a two-year gap in age between the boys. The younger boy certainly failed to match the unrealistic expectations and was beaten, ridiculed, scolded, criticised, negatively labelled and frequently compared to his brother. Now, an act of comparison is an act of rejection: it rejects the person who is being compared and puts pressure on the person to whom one is compared. The younger boy first came to my attention when he was sixteen years of age. He had already been labelled schizophrenic. During conversations with him I would notice his attention had wandered and I would ask, 'Where are you now?'. 'Oh, I'm a maths teacher in the best school in England and the A-level results just came out and my class has got the highest results in the whole of England.' This sad young man had hundreds of fantasies and lived most of the time in a fantasy world. He had begun this retreat into an imaginary world at five years of age. To label him 'schizophrenic' did not help as once again he experienced 'not being good enough'. His delusional world was a strategy to protect him from a very painful reality of parental rejection – hardly insanity!

A relevant question here is if one lives up to the condition for love does one achieve a fulfilling life? Not so, because one is always anxious about not measuring up. The life of the older brother of the boy being discussed brings home this point. He went on to do excellent A-levels and then on to university. At the end of his first university year he failed two components of his examinations. This was his first experience of academic failure and he knew well what the consequences would be when the news was brought home. What was he to do? Suicide was a high probability. Fortunately, he did not choose that path. However, he did not repeat the examinations in the autumn for two reasons: he was afraid he might fail again, and he was terrified that his parents would discover that he had failed already. The beginning of October came and a horrifying dilemma faced him. Keeping his secret he packed his bags and pretended he was heading back to university. For two years he lived alone in a bedsitter in Birmingham until he finally broke down under the strain of the pretence and fear of the consequences of discovery. Like his brother I met him in the admission ward of a psychiatric hospital.

❏ *Self-esteem and teacher training*

These observations are not meant as criticism of teachers. Indeed, the training programmes for teachers of both primary and secondary education leave a lot to be desired. All teachers know of the three Rs, but what about the three Is: initiation, induction and in-service?

■ Initiation

Our initiation into teaching certainly provided us with a reasonable grounding on *what to teach*. However, the *how to teach* was badly neglected. The how entails understanding the emotional, social, sexual, spiritual, physical, sensual and creative modes of human behaviour. It also includes knowledge of the effects of conflict on children in both the home and school and the means of resolving such conflict. A knowledge of communication processes is essential, particularly those processes that aid the development of self-esteem of students. The areas of staff development, staff cohesiveness and cooperation, stress management, whole-school approaches, leadership, conflict resolution among staff and basic counselling skills need also to be included in teacher training. The three main sources of stress in an increasingly pressurised teaching profession are role demands, difficult students and staff relationships. In my experience staff relationships are the greatest source of stress – this is true of many other professions as well. Many school staffs are characterised by cliques, resentments, rivalry, open hostility, hidden resentments, teachers isolated in their classrooms, autocratic leadership, poor morale, lack of cooperation, devisiveness on key issues, poor affirmation and hostile silences. These non-supportive environments reflect and have a detrimental effect on the self-esteem of each staff member. More sadly, they cast their shadows beyond the staffrooms into the classrooms. Again, this is not to blame teachers but to highlight the lack of training and consequent poor insight into these matters.

■ Induction

If initiation into teaching leaves a lot to be desired, induction is a total non-starter. My first experience of teaching in a second-level school was a major shock to my enthusiasm. The school was in north Dublin and dressed in a three-piece grey suit with leather briefcase, I walked down the corridors of the school to the students' whistling of the James Bond theme. I met the vice-principal, was presented with my timetable and shown to my classroom. When I looked through the glass into the classroom the students were throwing chairs and desks at each other. I visibly paled. Apparently, car tyre slashing was another favourite student occupation. The school was a veritable jungle. Not surprisingly, staff turnover was very high. There was no way my training equipped me to deal with these students' very obvious and deep social, emotional and behavioural problems. Most of the day went into attempts to control students. I approached the principal for advice, support, backup – plain and simple help. However, I was told that I was responsible for my own classes and any problems therein. I resigned after three weeks. I later found a job in the opposite type of school – that of overcontrol. That too had its problems but at least I felt safe. When I completed my doctorate training in clinical psychology I was still obliged to do two years of supervision under a senior clinical psychologist. A similar system is needed for young teachers. A two-year induction time under the supervision of a teacher with a minimum of five years' experience would benefit the novice teacher and provide formal recognition of the older teacher's experience. Principals of schools also would need to be sensitive to the needs and vulnerabilities of younger teachers during this induction period and provide advice, support and affirmation.

■ In-service training

The third 'I' is in-service training. All professions are in evolution and the need to stay abreast of developments in theory and practice is essential. Indeed, the process needs to be an integral part of a professional's life. Amazingly, this has not been the case within education. Certainly, many individual teachers, at their own expense, have pursued postgraduate courses but the Department of Education has only weakly endorsed and never financed or encouraged such development. Irish society has changed radically within the last twenty years. The rapid decline of religion, the massive rise in marital breakdown and separation, the increase in single-parent families, the influence of the media, the development of a more pluralist society, the unemployment crisis, changing values and morals – all of these changes influence what happens in schools. Twenty years ago discipline problems were a rare phenomenon in classrooms. Children were members of three main systems: the family, the school and the church. Authoritarianism ruled the day, and was predictably and consistently applied and reinforced across the three systems. Fear was the major weapon of control within the three systems. Whilst this approach was successful in effecting quiet it did not at all mean that learning was promoted: witness the high level of adult literacy and numeracy problems in this country. Furthermore, authoritarianism fosters passivity or, for some brave souls who rebel, aggression. Neither of these reactions are healthy for mature development. Parents and teachers need to educate children for responsibility and self-control – not control by others.

The decline in authoritarianism led to inconsistency between home and school systems which can be very confusing for both students and teachers. If, for example, a student from a democratic family system, which fosters self-control and responsibility, comes into a school which is authoritarian and fosters control by others, the student will be confused and sometimes reactionary. Furthermore, within any one school, the student may experience a democratic system in one classroom and an authoritarian one in another. Similarly, if a student comes from an authoritarian family system into a democratic school system, confusion will also result. Until a situation of predictability and consistency is established across the main systems of which children are members, discipline problems are likely to persevere and even escalate. Children will no longer accept authoritarianism, and rightly so! A democratic system that values each child as a unique human being, that heralds the capability of the child, that is affirmative, supportive, caring, fair, just and positively firm in the face of irresponsible behaviours must be developed within each major system. Predictability and consistency are hallmarks of any effective social system. Their importance underlies the developing awareness of the need for close liaison between homes and schools, and for whole-school approaches that emphasise effective interstaff communication, staff development and staff cohesiveness. No longer must a teacher be left isolated in the classroom to cope with the multiple emotional, behavioural, educational, sexual, social and spiritual problems of students. In-service training then needs to focus on a greater psychological and sociological understanding of student and teacher behaviour; effective responses to emotional, behavioural and social problems in students and professional colleagues; staff development in terms of effective communication systems; stress management; staff cohesiveness; problem-solving; more positive approaches to teaching; leadership styles; management systems and personal development.

❑ *Changing self-esteem*

There are two interdependent factors in personal change: *awareness* and *action*. Awareness of itself is not sufficient. Having identified your level of self-esteem, the conditions that you believe make for acceptance by others and self, and your use of introjecting and projecting styles of communication, you are now ready for change through the use of counter-conditioning behaviours.

The principal awareness is that behaviour does not determine your worth as a human being; behaviour is your means of experiencing this world and neither adds to nor detracts from your unique humanity. In the same vein, all behaviour has a function: failure and mistakes are means to further learning and growth, not statements about capability. Furthermore, any act of comparison of yourself with others is an act of rejection of self.

To change self-esteem entails using the same means that brought about your present level of value of self. As has been seen, it is the relationships you experienced with parents, teachers and other significant adults during your childhood that principally define your self-esteem. If the cause then of middle or poor self-esteem is relationships, the 'cure' must also be a relationship. However, as an adult your relationship with others will not raise self-esteem. Many adults continue to try to achieve security through their relationships with others but this is dependency and can lead to all types of problems in relationships (possessiveness, controlling, criticism, manipulation), to conflict and a further blow to self-esteem. The way to change your self-esteem is by means of a relationship with yourself. This relationship must have all the characteristics of a loving and affirmative parent–child relationship. It needs to be primarily *emotional* in nature so that all your thoughts and actions are infused with a valuing and celebration of self. Valuing and celebration must be an every-moment experience in your daily life so that the flood of affirming actions sweeps out the old tide of rejection of self, conditionality, negative thinking, avoidance of challenge, aggression or passivity, and neglect of physical well-being.

Change occurs by ensuring that all actions are of a self-valuing and self-caring nature, whether they have to do with rest, hygiene, driving, career, diet, relationships, physical exercise, lifestyle or school discipline. To rush and race, eat unhealthy foods, miss meals, rush meals, criticise oneself, compare oneself with others, be aggressive, accept aggression from others, be passive in the face of others, be manipulative, be irresponsible, be possessive, be controlling, overwork regularly, overindulge frequently in any food or beverage, never say 'no' to others, people-please at all times, look for approval from others – these are all examples of lack of value of self. Reverse the cycle: do everything calmly and in a relaxed manner, eat foods that nurture you, give yourself adequate time to eat and digest, listen to self, encourage yourself to do your best, see mistakes and failures as opportunities for learning, be assertive about your own views whilst respecting others, be spontaneous and open, be non-conformist, be honest, be unaccepting of any artificial goals that people may attempt to impose on you, be responsive to your own needs and to the reasonable needs of others, be moderate in your intake of food and beverages, be regular in physical exercise and balanced in your lifestyle in terms of allocating time to meeting your various needs. Balanced lifestyle is a good indicator of high self-esteem. It entails being responsive to all your needs – emotional, social, sexual, physical, behavioural (skills development), cognitive, spiritual, recreational and occupational. Another indicator of high self-esteem is being calm and relaxed, undefensive in the face of others' problematic behaviours.

Changing your concept of self is an endless process that needs to be consistently worked on at all times. The old rejecting and dependent ways are strongly ingrained and it is only through constant reinforcement of a cycle of accepting behaviours that these old damaging ways will be eradicated. The rewards are high: security, independence, freedom to be yourself, spontaneity, unconditionality with yourself and others, clear and direct in communication, peacefulness and tranquillity, openness to change, to others and to life, and increased potential for self-fulfilment.

Checklist for self-esteem enhancement	
How you relate to yourself in terms of the following behaviours will be a good indication of your level of self-esteem and how to enhance it. So, read through the list and note (say, on a scale of 0–5) how you relate to yourself for each of the behaviours.	
• Affirmation	• Positive self-talk
• Acceptance	• Supportive
• Praise	• Nurturance
• Encouragement	• Healthy diet
• Understanding	• Regular exercise
• Compassion	• Positive firmness
• Listening	• Responsible
• Valuing	• Kind
• Loving	• Caring
• Humorous	• Fair
• Challenging	• Belief in one's capability
• Relaxed	• Unconditionality
• Balanced lifestyle	

❑ *Changing communication patterns*

It has been pointed out already that a major give-away of self-esteem problems is the defensive communication patterns of introjection and projection. Introjection reveals identity confusion with other's opinions or feedback while projection indicates identity problems through passing the responsibility for your happiness and fulfilment in life onto others. When you introject or personalise, others will perceive you as being hypersensitive, easily hurt and vulnerable, and as somebody in need of protection. When you project, others will see you as dominating, aggressive, pushy or manipulative, passive, needy, dependent or passively aggressive. Both types of communication inevitably lead to conflict and a lowering of self-esteem.

Personalisation and projection arise from dependency on people for acceptance and approval with consequent fears of rejection, disapproval, criticism and failure. Dependency in turn arises from poor acceptance and valuing of self (middle to low self-esteem), which in turn arises from unresolved conflicts in childhood when either conditional parenting/teaching or total neglect left one feeling highly vulnerable. It is important to see this process clearly because reducing or overcoming personalisation and projection is only possible when all the aspects that have contributed to their development are perceived and worked upon.

As illustrated below, protective communication patterns are but the crest of a wave of an underlying sea of emotional experiences. Clearly, the more you correct your relationship with yourself (parenting self) so that you are unconditionally accepting of self, the more that each level of the problem hierarchy will become resolved. The more you elevate your self-esteem the more you reduce dependency on others, extinguish fears and become separate from parents and others. When that happens, your communication patterns will automatically change. However, the process of self-change is a long one and in the meantime it is useful to become more aware of destructive styles of communication and to replace them with more constructive methods.

Introjection and projection

↕

Fears of rejection, failure, criticism

↕

**Dependence on others
for acceptance and approval**

↕

Middle to poor self-esteem
(poor acceptance and valuing of self)

↕

Unresolved childhood conflicts
(due to either conditional parenting/teaching
or total parental neglect)

■ Introjection

Like any other process of change, awareness and action are the key elements. Recognising the tendency to introject, to person-alise other people's behaviours as saying something about self, is the first step to changing that misinterpretation. The second step is the awareness that no matter what another person says or does it is a statement about that person. The first internal action to take when, for example, a person sends you a 'you' message, like 'you're insensitive', is to ask yourself quickly, 'what is this saying about the person addressing me?', and then return the message to that person in order to get to the hidden 'I' message. In the present example the best way to return the 'you' message is to say, 'in what way do you find me insensitive?' The answer might be another 'you' message, like 'you're never here for me' or 'you're always out' or 'you never listen'. So, once again you bat back the message by saying – taking the examples given – 'in what way do you need me here for you?' or 'do you want me home more often?' or 'what am I not hearing from you?' Communication has stayed open and the 'I' messages will now begin to emerge, such as 'I am lonely and need more contact with you' or 'I need to go out socially with you' or 'I need for you to hear my opinions and needs'.

What is clear now is that the original 'you' messages (projections by the other person) hid 'I' messages about blocked needs. If you had personalised these messages and had either withdrawn or attacked back, communication would have broken down, the relationship would have suffered, both persons would have gone away hurt and bruised, and the blocked needs would have remained unmet. At least when needs are expressed there is an opportunity to explore whether you are in a position to meet them. If the needs are reasonable then a 'yes' is generally in order, if unreasonable, then a 'no' is in order, if the needs are somewhat difficult to meet then negotiation may be necessary. What is important is that all the time you have held on to your own value in yourself and have stayed separate but caring in your response to the other person's communication.

Steps to reducing introjection

1. Awareness of tendency to personalise.
2. Awareness that verbal and non-verbal communications are entirely about the person addressing you.
3. Internal action: 'what's this saying about the person sending the message?'
4. Return message to sender in order to discover the hidden 'I' message.
5. Hold on to your value and acceptance of self.
6. Respond appropriately to revealed blocked needs.
7. Affirm your need to keep communication open at all times.

■ Projection

As illustrated earlier, projection is only the crest of the wave when it comes to understanding the turbulent seas of human vulnerability. Nonetheless, as with introjection, it is necessary to take charge and change this destructive means of relating to others. The initial steps are similar to those for changing personalisation: awareness of tendency to project, and awareness that all behaviour coming from you is about you, that others are not responsible for you. The first internal action is owning all aspects of self. Below is an affirmation exercise which highlights the absolute need of adults to own everything about themselves.

Declaration of my uniqueness

⊃ I wonder at my unique being.

⊃ I am a once-off happening in this universe that will never reoccur.

⊃ I love, value, celebrate and own everything about me.

⊃ I love and care for my body which carries every aspect of me. I will nurture, exercise, rest and accept every aspect of my body. I do not want my body to be like anybody else's.

⊃ I love, value and wonder at the limitless capacity of my mind.

⊃ I own my mistakes and failures and realise these do not in any way take away from my wondrous capacity. I see mistakes and failures purely as opportunities for further learning.

⊃ I enjoy my achievements and successes but do not hold on to any of them as indicators of my worth. My worth and value are independent of all my actions.

⊃ I strongly distinguish between my being and my behaviour.

⊃ I am unconditional in my regard for myself and others.

⊃ No action on the part of myself or others takes away from my worth, value and uniqueness.

⊃ I own and take responsibility for all my thoughts, images, ambitions, words and actions, whether they be of a positive or negative nature and whether they be towards others or myself.

⊃ There are many things I have done or may do that I regret or will regret but I am determined to grow from these experiences and learn to love myself and others more deeply every day.

⊃ I will be honest and open about behaviour that is distressful to me but in a way that does not put the other person down.

⊃ Equally, I will be open and listen to what others have to say to me about what behaviours of mine they find distressful and I will take responsibility for any neglect or hurt I may have caused.

⊃ No matter what happens I will not cease to care for myself or others.

⊃ I know I have immense abilities to grow and develop in this world. I can touch, see, feel, hear, think, imagine, say and do. I can be deeply close to others. I can be productive. I can make sense and meaning of what often seems an uncaring and cruel world.

⊃ I will always remain true to my uniqueness and not allow others to impose artificial goals upon me.

⊃ I am unique, perfect in my being and, once I remain in possession of my wondrous being, I can create a better world for me and others.

When you project you put the responsibility for your life onto another. For example, if you say, 'you make me miserable' or 'you never consult me' or 'you never consider me', you are giving a lot of power over to the person you are addressing and you are abrogating your own responsibility for your own needs. In communicating with another, you need to first own your needs and then send an 'I' message about some need you have. Taking the examples above, you might say: 'when I'm left alone every evening I feel miserable and lonely and I would like more time with you' or 'I would like to be consulted on issues related to my work in this school' or 'I would like my needs to develop my career to be considered'. Having expressed your need, the next step is to accept that your message is not a command but a request; therefore you have to allow the other person the right to say 'yes' or 'no' to your need without either response affecting your value and respect for the other person or for yourself. Remember that you own your own needs and meeting those needs is your responsibility.

Steps to overcoming projection

1. Recognition of tendency to use projection as a means of getting your needs in life met.
2. Awareness that projection is a mirror of your dependency on others.
3. Own everything about yourself.
4. Send an 'I' message regarding an unmet need.
5. Allow the receiver the freedom to say 'yes' or 'no' to an expressed need (whether reasonable, unreasonable or difficult).
6. Take responsibility for getting your own needs met.

A good question is what do you do when reasonable needs – for example, for a student to be responsible and orderly in class, for a principal to support you in classroom management issues or for a partner to respond to your sexual needs – are consistently not being met? You must hold on to the realisation that you cannot force another (whether through aggression, manipulation or withdrawal) to meet your needs. Unfortunately, the reverse often happens and accounts for much conflict within relationships, staffrooms and classrooms. The first step is to enquire from the person concerned what is it that blocks her from meeting what you believe is a reasonable need. In actively listening to her response you might discover that she has some deeper, even more expedient need than yours that is not being met. Again, taking the examples above, you might find that the student who is uncooperative has a massive unmet need to be valued by others; or your principal lacks confidence, is threatened by failure and has an unmet need for acceptance from staff members; or your partner, who is not responsive to your sexual needs, has an unmet emotional need for you to be affectionate at other times than just in bed. If you respond to the unmet need of the other person you will often find that that person then becomes more disposed towards meeting your needs. By staying open to the other person, in spite of her not meeting your need, you facilitate positive movement and growth in the relationship where hidden needs are revealed and, when reasonable, met. Sometimes, it will arise that the other person is seriously blocked within herself and so, in spite of your repeated attempts to discover the blocked needs, she remains closed off to your understanding and to your needs. Such a person needs professional help to move out of a subconsciously 'stuck' position. The important point to bear in mind is that her being blind to your worth is a message about her not about you.

When you first begin to work on being more positive and independent in your communication with others, you may fail more often than you succeed, as old patterns die hard. Persist and the gains will be a more valuing relationship with yourself and others.

❏ *Key insights*
- Personal and professional effectiveness are strongly related to one's level of self-esteem.
- The causes of self-esteem lie principally in the early experiences of childhood within the home and school.
- In teacher training, the 'how to teach' needs as much emphasis as the 'what to teach'.

- Continual updating of theory and practice must be an integral part of a teacher's career.
- Person and behaviour are separate issues.
- Conditionality breeds neuroses and, in extreme cases, psychoses.
- Staying separate is the key to effective relationships.
- Personalisation (introjection) is a misinterpretation of another person's behaviour as saying something about oneself and leads to conflict and breakdown of communication.
- Projection involves transferring responsibility for one's own needs onto others and leads, ultimately, to conflict and communication breakdown.
- Both personalisation and projection are indicators of dependence on others and middle or poor self-esteem.
- There are two interdependent factors in personal change: awareness and action.

❏ *Key actions*

- Identify your own level of self-esteem.
- Identify and free yourself of the conditions you set for acceptance and valuing of yourself by self and others.
- Recognise and correct your use of introjecting and projecting styles of protective communication.
- Ensure that all your actions are of a self-valuing and self-caring nature.
- Unconditionally accept and value yourself.

CHAPTER 3

The Staffroom

❏ *Staff relationships*
❏ *Communication and staff relationships*
  ▪ Protective communication
    ↬ **Judgmental**
    ↬ **Controlling**
    ↬ **Strategic**
    ↬ **Neutral**
    ↬ **Superior**
    ↬ **Certain**
  ▪ Open communication
  ▪ Expression of needs
❏ *Seeking and receiving staff support*
  ▪ 'Weakness' is strength
  ▪ Welfare and emergency feelings
  ▪ Dependence versus independence
❏ *Staff morale*
  ▪ Staff interaction
  ▪ Decision-making
  ▪ Availability of leaders
  ▪ Affirmation of staff
  ▪ Constructive feedback on differences
  ▪ Affirmation of leaders
❏ *Problem-solving*
❏ *Responding to rigidity in self and others*
❏ *Key insights*
❏ *Key actions*

❏ *Staff relationships*

My experience of working in schools over many years now suggests that staff relationships are rarely of a healthy, open, cooperative and dynamic nature. The contrary is usually the case: rivalry, hostility, cliques, gossip, resentment, isolation, fear, aggression, dependency, criticism and alienation abound.

41

As has been already pointed out, staff relationships are a major contributor to stress in teaching. This is not good for a profession that so needs the back-up of colleagues to deal with the rising tide of stressors within it. However, teaching as a profession is quite defensive and slow to be influenced by either progressive people within the profession or professionals outside it. One reason for this is that many teachers' identities are tied up subconsciously with their professional performance, and any feedback or suggestions for change are read as threats to self-esteem, thereby giving rise to defensive behaviours of denial, non-cooperation, non-listening or hostility.

It should be of interest to all members of staff when a colleague has a self-esteem problem, as the manifestations of it are likely to affect all relationships and activities within the school. The teacher with low self-esteem may be the passive, quiet teacher who works extremely hard, putting immense pressure on himself and very often on students, but making no demands of his colleagues. Frequently this teacher may have control difficulties within the classroom. However, he does not seek help from colleagues and the problems continue to escalate. On the other hand, a teacher with low self-esteem may also manifest inner conflicts through an overbearing, aggressive manner. This teacher may use authoritarian control methods and can sometimes be both verbally and physically violent. At staff meetings he may be uncooperative, dominating and abusive of anyone who does not see things his way. All these maladaptive behaviours are a screen to a very great underlying insecurity.

Both of these teachers have a similar underlying problem of self-esteem. The dominant, aggressive teacher tries to get approval and acceptance by compelling these responses from others. The passive, unassertive teacher gains approval by being the 'people-pleaser' always trying to meet the needs of others. Both, however, make for a difficult staff environment as they are highly sensitive to feedback and resistant to change. Nonetheless, it is important that all staff be concerned to create a supportive and positive environment so that colleagues with self-esteem difficulties (which we all have to some degree) may find the safety to express their needs and concerns and get the help they need to resolve their inner conflicts. One of the primary means of establishing positive staff relationships is mature communication.

❏ *Communication and staff relationships*

There are two main types of communication: open and protective. Unfortunately, the type of communication that is most used in many staffrooms, not just school staffrooms, is protective communication. This creates relationship problems and damages the self-esteem of staff members. As you read the descriptions below you may be surprised to discover how rarely you use open/relating communication patterns and how often you use protective communication patterns.

▪ Protective communication

Protective patterns of communication block mature contact between staff members and produce a circular reaction of protectiveness. They lead to an unsupportive and threatening environment. Protective communication takes many forms.

↝ Judgmental

When a teacher is judgmental he accuses and criticises which results in a protective response from the other person of either withdrawal or a criticism in return.

Examples:

- Criticising, name calling, characterising, blaming (e.g. 'You're a fool', 'You never listen', 'You're a typical teacher').
- Cross-examining, interrogating, fact-finding (e.g. 'Are you sure you know what you're talking about?', 'Are you telling me the truth?').
- Praising and approving (e.g. 'You're a great teacher', 'You prepared a good agenda for the meeting', 'That's a brilliant piece of work').

Many people have difficulty in grasping that praising and approving can have negative effects on relationships and on self-esteem. When these messages are sent they are generally well intended (unless there is a hidden agenda, then they are manipulative) but when they are phrased as in the examples above they imply that the sender can judge the other's performance. They also raise the possibility that the next performance may be disapproved of, perhaps only by failure to show approval. The relationship created is that of judge–supplicant. Does that mean you should never praise or approve others' performances? Certainly not, but there are two issues to be considered here. First, it is always better to put the emphasis on effort rather than performance, as every effort is an attainment. Second, when praise or approval is expressed in a judgmental way – 'you're a great lad' – it expresses nothing about the sender and therefore it is a distorted message. Recall that all communications are about the sender. Therefore, it is far more accurate when communicating that you are impressed by, for example, a person's work or dress or grasp of a subject, to say 'I am impressed by your essay' or 'I like the colours you are wearing' or 'I am in awe of your grasp of this subject'. The 'I' message communicates something about your perception but allows the other to evaluate her own performance. Indeed, it is often wise when you wish to communicate your perception of another's behaviour that you first ask how that person sees it.

⇨ Controlling

When a teacher is controlling he is authoritarian, threatening and moralistic – all of which produce reactions of either fright or fight; certainly protectiveness; either acquiescence or resistance; and always resentment. The teacher who is controlling does not listen to the other's opinions or views and discounts that person's feelings. Depending on the nature of the receiver these types of communication can produce either aggression or passivity, rebelliousness or acquiescence, fearfulness or authoritarianism. Controlling messages implicitly communicate that the receiver is unable to be responsible for herself and is in need of a controller, who, of course, is attempting to boost, in vain, his own self-esteem at the expense of another. It therefore damages the self-esteem of the receiver, creates protectiveness in the relationship and does nothing for the self-development of the sender.

Examples:

- Directing, commanding, ordering (e.g. 'Do what you're told', 'Get down to your work', 'You must change').
- Warning, threatening, punishing (e.g. 'If you bring up that I'll never talk to you again', 'You'd better do what I say').
- Moralising, preaching ('Good people don't support divorce', 'Do you know what you should do with your life', 'Teachers should be able to control their classes').

⇨ Strategic

In this type of protective communication the sender has hidden motivations – better known as 'hidden agendas' – and is strategically attempting to manipulate the other into meeting some hidden needs. It is akin to emotional blackmail except that it is happening at a covert level. If the receiver responds to the manipulation she will be heartily reinforced but if she refuses to cooperate, outright rejection can speedily occur. The person who engages in manipulation has low self-esteem, otherwise he would be open about needs and willing to accept whatever response the receiver would give. The strategy is to reduce risk so that failure is minimised and no humiliation is experienced. However, this approach undermines the relationship between the two people as no openness, trust or genuineness is shown and it also weakens the self-esteem of the other.

Examples:

- Non-verbal manipulation: sulking, withdrawing, hostile silences, sighing.
- Verbal manipulation (e.g. 'If you do that for me, I'll look after you', 'Nobody sees how hard I have to work here').

⇨ Neutral

When a teacher is neutral in communicating he shows little concern for the other person. Somehow the teacher is threatened by either emotional closeness or emotional conflict, and neutrality protects against venturing into affective areas or ways of relating that threaten self-esteem. Very often the teacher manifests the 'being busy' syndrome to protect himself against rejection. Unfortunately, because the other does not read the sender's neutrality as a protective device she can feel hurt, dismissed, unwanted and of little value. Once again the self-esteem of both parties and the relationship between them are weakened.

Examples:

- Withdrawing, diverting (e.g. 'I won't discuss it any further', 'That is the end of the matter').
- Ignoring, dismissing, responding 'on the run' (e.g. 'Don't be bothering me with that', 'Can't stop now, must run').
- Reassuring, excusing, consoling, sympathising (e.g. 'Time cures everything', 'I'm sure he's not saying what you think he's saying').
- Me-too messages (e.g. 'Didn't I have that trouble too', 'Don't I know exactly how you feel').

⇨ **Superior**

Basically the message being sent here is that 'I know best' or 'I am right' and 'if you follow my advice you won't go wrong'. The person who communicates in this superior way is. in reality, masking an inferiority complex. The need to be superior is an attempt to gain acceptance and approval from others. In reality it has the opposite effect as superiority deprives the receiver of the esteem-building experience of solving her own problems. It also encourages dependency in the receiver (which the sender needs in order to feel good) and it very often leads to conflict (e.g. the receiver responds 'Don't tell me how to lead my life'). A very wise rule of thumb is never to give advice to an adolescent or adult unless they request it.

Examples:

- Advising, recommending (e.g. 'What you should do is . . . ', 'Why don't you leave teaching?').
- Diagnosing, psychoanalysing (e.g. 'You're only saying that because you're tired', 'You just don't like men, do you?', 'It's just your period time').

↝ **Certain**

The certain type of communication is common in teachers who possess very rigid attitudes and who tend to live their lives according to 'shoulds', 'should nots', 'musts' and 'ought tos'. (Rigidity is discussed in more detail later – see pp. 68–71.) The need to be dogmatic and certain is again a means to gain acceptance and approval. To reveal any uncertainty and provisionalism in this teacher's eyes would be to show vulnerability and weakness, and to risk disapproval. This type of communication does not value the other person's differences from the sender; indeed it emphasises the receiver's 'wrongness', invalidates her feelings and leads to protectiveness and lack of openness.

Examples:

- Persuading, lecturing, arguing (e.g. 'I am absolutely right about this', 'The fact is . . . ', 'There is only one way to do this').

Protective communication patterns are reflective of non-supportive environments, where the self-esteem of staff members is frequently threatened, leading to lack of openness and trust, and poor staff relationships.

■ Open communication

Open communication is exactly the opposite of protective communication.

Protective communication	Open communication
Judgmental	Non-judgmental
Controlling	Permissive (allows the other person freedom to see and do things own way)
Strategic	Spontaneous
Neutral	Empathic (attempts to see and feel what the other person is experiencing)
Superior	Equal (respects and listens to the other person's opinions and ways of doing things)
Certain	Provisional (accepts that there may be an alternative answer or way)

Open communication, a rare phenomenon, is essential for the fulfilment of individual and staff goals. It is a style of communication where each is aware of and experiences openness, closeness and understanding of the other, and what is discussed is pertinent, relevant and appropriate. To engage in this type of relating you need to have high self-esteem, a feeling of adequacy and competency, and trust in your ability to assist another. You also need to be aware of your weaknesses and vulnerabilities, and be able to reveal them when expedient. This can only occur within a supportive staff environment.

It is incumbent on all staff members to practise communication patterns that create positive, open, caring, and trusting relationships, not only within the staffroom but also within the classroom as children tend to imitate the communication behaviours of significant adults in their lives. Good staff morale makes it easier to establish a supportive staff environment. The real key to healthy staff relationships is where each member works to establish a high level of self-esteem.

■ Expression of needs

Communication is principally about needs: when it is protective people's needs are rarely met; when it is open needs are generally well met.

There are, in effect, four ways you can express a need. One way is to be *direct and clear*. For example, your principal has made a decision about your work and has not consulted you about it. You feel angry as you have a need to be consulted on matters affecting your responsibilities. You want to send a direct and clear message to John the school principal: 'John, (direct) when decisions are made about my work without consultation with me, I feel angry and I'm asking that in future I be consulted on such matters'. This kind of message is a rare phenomenon. What is more likely is that one of the following kinds of message is sent:

- indirect but clear
- direct but unclear
- indirect and unclear.

Taking the example above, and using the *indirect but clear* mode, the message now becomes: 'People (indirect) who make decisions about other people's work make me angry'. John, the principal, can totally ignore this message as it is not addressed to him and he has no responsibility for deciphering your twisted messages. It is your responsibility to send a direct and clear message.

The most typical way we communicate is in the *direct but unclear* mode so that the message to John now becomes: 'John, you think you can do what you like in this school'. This message is certainly directed to John – indeed there is a surfeit of 'yous' – but the content is totally masked. John does not know what your outburst is all about. Regrettably, we are all masters of the 'you' message which says nothing at all about the sender, and thus the real message lies hidden. As was noted earlier, messages are entirely about the sender. A 'you' message, then, is protective and leads to either attack or flight on the part of the receiver. A typical defensive retort to the direct but unclear message in the example above is: 'You're always complaining about something'. Communication has now broken down as both parties are engaging in problematic communication patterns.

The final type of communication, *indirect and unclear*, is totally distorted and leads to all types of relationship problems. Cynicism and sarcasm are examples of this pattern. In the present example the message becomes: 'People can be so full of you know what'.

The only healthy way to communicate is to use the direct and clear statement, making sure that the message is an 'I' and not a 'you' message. 'You' messages are judgmental, critical, superior or certain, and they damage self-esteem. 'I' messages, on the other hand, are a total owning of one's own needs or perceptions and put no pressure on the other party to respond. As a result, the likelihood of communication remaining open is greater. All the time the communicator is respecting and valuing his colleague; is accepting the colleague's right to be different in outlook, philosophy and attitudes; and is allowing his colleague the freedom to respond or not to respond.

Practice of direct and clear communication creates a supportive staffroom environment.

❏ *Seeking and receiving staff support*

There are factors other than communication that contribute to the development of a healthy staffroom climate. One such factor is seeking and receiving the help and support of colleagues. Again this behaviour is not common but when you look at the three requirements that need to be present for teachers to go to one another for support, you will understand what blocks the development of such mature consultation. The three requirements are:

- an understanding that seeking and receiving support is a necessary strength required for reducing stress and that this needs to become part of the daily working routine
- an ability to value and respect your own feelings, to be able to identify them and talk them through in full openness
- an ability to be vulnerable, to trust and to receive the time, attention and care of another person.

■ 'Weakness' is strength

The first requirement runs counter to what most of us learned: do not show weakness or vulnerability, and do not ask for help. Indeed, many see asking for help as a weakness. The problem is that every time you suppress the need for support and help you miss the chance to grow. St Paul said it very well: 'When I am weak, I am strong'. It is through accepting your weaknesses that you grow in strength and knowledge and ability to cope. There is much expertise, wisdom, support, understanding and counsel available in any staffroom but it is seldom utilised. A young teacher can gain much from an older teacher. A teacher having problems with a particular class can get advice from a teacher who is having no problems with that class – clearly, what the latter is doing works and what the former is doing does not. Likewise, all teachers can gain from a sharing and a pooling of resources to deal with the most problematic students. The teacher left isolated with such students is unlikely to be successful. Many teachers are fearful of going to colleagues for help as they think that their colleagues will feel they should not be teaching if they are not able to cope. Unfortunately, in some cases their fears are not without

ground. So, certainly the safety of not being judged or criticised is important if teachers are to be able to go to each other
for help. Nevertheless, you need to get to a place of independence of the responses of colleagues and to be determined to
grow from every vulnerability and weakness that arises.

■ Welfare and emergency feelings

The second requirement is concerned with expression of feelings which are the kernel of any communication. The difficulty
is that most people do not value their feelings, particularly
feelings like fear, anger, sadness, resentment, jealousy and guilt.
They see these feelings as 'bad' or 'negative', while feelings like
love, comfort, joy, confidence and enthusiasm are seen as 'good'
or 'positive'. If you view certain feelings as negative then expression of them is difficult because of your own negative attitude
and the threat of other people also seeing them in the same
negative way. Many people even have difficulty in expressing
the so-called 'positive' feelings as they fear rejection. Men, in
particular, are not good at expressing 'good' feelings as stereotyping in childhood led to the inhibition of such feelings.
Stereotyping has been kinder to women as generally they are
much better at expressing all feelings except anger. As a result
women tend to be physically healthier than men and outlive
men by an average of eight years. Research has shown that men
who over a long period of time persistently suppress or repress
their feelings of grief, sadness, resentment, fear, threat and so
on are very prone to cardiovascular disease. Recent research
indicates that women who, for background reasons other than
stereotyping, 'bottle up' feelings such as anger, loneliness and
fear are prone to breast cancer. Inability to express hostility is
also strongly associated with certain cancers.

It is important to emphasise that there are no such things
as 'negative' or 'bad' feelings. As you will see all feelings are
positive. Rather than the terms positive and negative, I prefer
to use the terms *welfare feelings* and *emergency feelings*: the
former refers to the so-called 'good' feelings and the latter to
the misnamed 'negative' feelings. Welfare feelings are well
named as they indicate that you are in a 'welfare state' or you
are experiencing a state of well-being. Emergency feelings are

even more aptly labelled as they indicate that you are in an 'emergency' state and some action is needed to return you to a state of well-being. Emergency feelings like fear and anger alert you to the need for emotional healing in the same way that physical pain alerts you to the need for physical healing. Both the emergency feeling and the physical pain are positive and necessary to recognise the need for action that will bring about a state of either emotional or physical well-being.

It is also wise to see that you cannot hurt yourself or others with feelings. For example, many people, particularly women, have difficulties in expressing anger. But anger is a feeling and it cannot hurt another person. However, actions hurt, whether verbal, non-verbal, written or physical. To express anger through aggression is abusive of another. But it is the action of aggression not the angry feeling that abuses the other. Anger is positive: it alerts you to some emergency situation and it gives you the energy to act on that situation. When you feel anger exploding within you it is best to reduce its power to a manageable proportion before expressing it as otherwise it may express itself through aggression. Aggression, of its very nature, puts the other person down, breaks communication and leaves the issue unresolved. The best way to reduce built-up, unmanageable anger is through some type of physical activity. Also, in this situation it is always wise to remove yourself from the target (student, child, spouse, colleague, friend) of your anger. Remember your anger is a revelation about some unmet need of yours which needs to be expressed in an assertive, direct and clear way using an 'I' message. It is not a message about the other person.

People rarely own, respect and value their feelings as expressions of unmet needs. The tendency of most of us is to suppress or to project emergency feelings through aggression ('You're the one who makes me miserable'), passive manipulation ('After all I have done for you and now you treat me in this way') or non-verbal manipulation such as hostile silences and sulking. There is a far more serious subconscious response to feelings (either welfare or emergency) and that is repression. People who repress do not consciously realise that they are cutting off their feelings. Very often these people go around with a placid, smiling appearance – they do not seem to react to expressions of welfare or emergency feelings from others and do not express these feelings themselves.

An example comes from a teacher who came to me for help with an obsessive-compulsive problem of having to check and recheck regulators (light switches, taps, cooker switches) many times before going to bed at night or before leaving the house in the morning. Her main preoccupation was with taps, but the compulsion had generalised to other regulators. The rationale that the teacher gave for her 'irrational' behaviour was that 'I'm afraid of flooding the house'. It took her hours to get to bed every night and frequently she would have to get out of the bed to recheck again. Similarly, in the mornings she rose early in order to go through her checking rituals and often had to return home when half-way to school. She was in her early thirties and had had no heterosexual relationship to date. Neither did she have any close female friends. What eventually emerged was that she had enormous fear of the expression of any feelings, whether of love or of fear and anger, as these feelings were not expressed by her parents when she was a child. Neither could her parents receive any such feelings. As a child she learned that her security rested on repression of all feelings. Her acceptability then depended on her being 'emotionless'. But feelings arise spontaneously and at thirty years of age she now had a huge flood of repressed feelings within her, needing to be seen and responded to, but which subconsciously were seen as life-threatening. It was not 'flooding the house' that accounted for her compulsive behaviour but 'the flood of emotions' within her. As she gradually learned to express the different feelings, the obsessive-compulsive behaviours began to extinguish.

The tormented life of people with obsessive-compulsive problems is illustrated in the following poem.

Compulsions

Checking, checking, checking,
twisting, twisting, twisting,
tight, tight, tight,
faster, faster, faster,

ah! all is right
no, no, check again
just one more run,
back, back, back,
lights, doors, taps,
switches, windows, gas.

Sleep, sleep, sleep,
ease, ease, ease,
no don't doze,
rise up once more,
no flood, no waste,
no light, no fire,
no flow,
no row,
no openness,
emotionless,
or world will cease.

Washing, washing, washing,
scrubbing, scrubbing, scrubbing,
five times,
how many times
no start again
one, two, three,
four, five, see
criss cross,
up and down
step missed
start again
skin raw, raw
bleeding, bleeding, bleeding,
no matter
do over and over.

Rubbing, rubbing, rubbing,
safe, safe, safe,
clean, clean, clean,
who sat there
did he touch there
did I touch here
wash, wash, wash,
scrub, scrub, scrub,
rash, rash, rash,

dirt, dirt, dirt,
unclean, unclean, unclean,
worthless, worthless, worthless,
never ending search,
spotless, spotless, spotless,
hateful, hateful, hateful
impure, impure, impure
who could ever love me?

You can now see that the second requirement for giving and receiving staff support is complex and that most of us have difficulties in the expression of both welfare and emergency feelings. Nonetheless, the way forward is the awareness that all feelings are positive, and that owning, valuing, respecting and constructively expressing feelings will lead to a resolution of personal and interpersonal issues.

■ Dependence versus independence

There is a notion about that never asking for help means being independent and that to do the contrary means being dependent. Is this true? Hardly. Since many of your needs are met in relationships – such as the need for affection, support, knowledge, expertise, advice, warmth, friendship, companionship and sexual gratification – it is a matter of survival and personal development that you express these needs. When you do not ask for support or help, then, surely this is an act of neglect of self? Ask yourself what is it that blocks you from making a request: is it fear of rejection, of being judged, criticised or disapproved of? If it is then your reticence is an act of dependence and not at all one of independence. Independence means making the request for support or whatever you want and being independent of the response of the receiver. For example, if you make a request of someone but expect him to say 'yes' and react negatively when he says 'no', then you are being dependent on him, expecting him to take responsibility for you. Remember a request is not a command. When you are independent you want the other person to be free to respond to your request and you value his 'no' in the same way as you would value his 'yes' response. Independence is being able to seek and receive help and support but allowing the other person freedom of response. Dependence, on the other hand, means either not expressing the need for help or support, or asking in a commanding rather than requesting manner. It is interesting that when you ask people how they feel when somebody asks for help, the usual response is 'I feel pleased and affirmed to be asked'. But when you reverse the question – 'Do you go to others for help?' – the usual response is 'no' because the expectation of how others will receive the request does not mirror people's own experience of being pleased when someone approaches them.

In all relationships it is important that we go to each other for care, affirmation, advice and support. It is even more important within the context of a stressful occupation that mutual support and help becomes an everyday experience. Within any staff group there are huge resources of help, creativity, wisdom, support and affirmation available; the sad thing is that such resources often lie untapped.

❏ *Staff morale*

The bedrock of a supportive staff environment is staff morale. Staff morale is the lifeblood of any staff group. Its promotion is the responsibility of all members of staff but it is particularly important that principals and vice-principals be active in its development; without their visible encouragement and participation it is unlikely to develop.

There are six main requirements for the creation of positive staff morale:

- high level of interaction among staff
- decisions are made by the group
- leaders are available and approachable
- leaders affirm staff and staff affirm each other
- constructive feedback on differences
- staff affirm leaders.

■ Staff interaction

The first requirement indicates that the more interaction that occurs between staff, the better the morale. Some staffs have a situation where members pass each other like ships in the night, never interacting. The more varied the interactions the better: social, problem-solving, support, affirmation, planning, care, creative, sport. It is important that the principal notices the teacher who absents himself from such interactions. Generally, such withdrawal is indicative of vulnerability and feelings of threat; a discreet, caring, concerned approach to this teacher is needed. Equally, the teacher who overdominates staff interactions needs to be delicately approached. Both of these teachers can unwittingly make the development of good staff morale difficult. Both need help and understanding.

■ Decision-making

The second requirement centres on decision-making. I once mentioned to a group of over 500 primary school teachers that my experience in going around to many schools was that some principals hid themselves away in their offices and class-rooms and only emerged to give instructions and commands, and that staff meetings were a rare phenomenon. There was a loud cheer from the audience which suggested that my obser-vation was not unfounded. It is also the experience of some staff that when staff meetings are convened, decisions have already been made by the principal before he comes to the meeting and that they are not included in the decision-making. This is an unwise practice as decisions which have not evolved from consultation with staff are likely to receive poor coopera-tion and can sometimes be sabotaged, and rightly so! Decisions which are not inclusive of staff are abusive and non-respecting of the staff's right to be participants in the decision-making process. Decisions which arise from joint decision-making are far more likely to be acted upon as staff members feel they are part of that decision and feel affirmed and respected by the consultation process. Regular, well-organised, goal-directed staff meetings are a must for the creation of good morale. Meetings for the sake of meetings only create frustration and annoyance, and weaken morale.

■ Availability of leaders

Effective leadership is an essential aspect of an effective school and is dealt with in more detail in Chapter 6. It has relevance

here in that availability and approachability of the principal
and vice-principal are important factors in the creation of
positive staff morale. Many principals complain that one of
their major tasks is dealing with a demoralised teaching staff
who have lost motivation and initiative, and who are no longer
challenged within their profession. Not an easy task! It is important that principals give very clear non-verbal and verbal messages of availability. Apart from crisis situations it is good to
specify times that are most convenient. Even more important
is communicating approachability. Non-verbal language speaks
volumes in this issue: lack of eye contact, talking 'on the run',
hasty conversations, clock-watching, irritability, severe facial
expressions, restlessness – all send messages of unapproachability. Further indicators of unapproachability include not
listening, not showing interest in colleagues' personal lives,
not exhibiting concern during staff members' personal or
professional crises, not delegating, not seeking colleagues'
opinions, not seeking help for self, blaming, criticising, not
relating on first-name terms. Approachability is conveyed
through good eye contact, listening, being concerned, being
sensitive to the stresses and strains teachers may be experiencing, spending personal time with each member of staff,
requesting support and help, admitting one's own vulnerabilities and actively responding to teachers' requests for help
and support.

▪ Affirmation of staff

The fourth requirement is affirmation of staff. Because few of
us have reached the peaks of high self-esteem affirmation from
colleagues and leaders aids the growth of self-esteem. Even
when you have high self-esteem, affirmation is a bonus to be
enjoyed. So, most of us have needs for recognition and approval.
The difficulty arises if the needs are dependency needs; criticism
and the absence of affirmation then become severe blows to self-
esteem, and, in turn, badly affect staff morale. Recognition,
respect, valuing, affirming, encouragement and praise are not
regular features of staff–staff or leader–staff interactions. What
is more common is criticism, avoidance, silence, negative
gossip and 'put-down' messages, all of which damage self-

esteem and staff morale. It is the responsibility of all members of staff and, again, especially leaders, to develop the art of affirmation. Giving affirmation is a subtle, delicate issue but when done well has many rewarding consequences. The following guidelines for giving affirmations should help you.

- *Only ever give honest and genuine affirmations.* If you are not genuine and sincere about a positive affirmation and you do not really feel that the person deserves it, your non-verbal language will give you away and your affirmation will be rejected as insincere.

- *Give an affirmation without expectation of a receptive response.* Generally it is true to say that when a person reacts defensively to a positive affirmation it means that the person needs more affirmations. Do not give up – remember that affirmation is an expression of something you feel and perceive, and must not be given to gain a particular response. In the end the other person will see your genuineness and be affirmed by it.

- *The best affirmation is undivided attention to the other person.* Avoid effusive compliments (they are rarely genuine). A look, a nod or a smile may be sufficient to affirm a colleague. Always be sure full attention is given.

- *Be sure the affirmation is unconditional and has no ulterior motive.* Do not give an affirmation to get something back (like an affirmation in return, praise or a favour) – that is manipulation and not affirmation.

- *Give affirmations frequently to create a cycle of affirming between staff members.*

- *Do not employ clichés, jargon and popular superlatives* ('Great!', 'Super!', 'Terrific!', 'A1!'); be yourself and be genuine.

- *Spontaneous unconditional affirmations are the most powerful.*

- *Focus your affirmations on an area that is important to your colleague.* Look for signs from the person of what is important to him. Possible considerations are dress, work, verbal language, body language, origin, social, cultural and educational background, knowledge of a specific topic, interests, hobbies, social behaviour. Listen also to what you hear from the students, colleagues, friends and partner of the person to whom you want to give affirmations.

■ Constructive feedback on differences

Feedback on differences between you and a colleague is easier to give and more likely to be received within a context of regular mutual affirmation. Giving positive affirmations generally comes more easily to people than communicating on differences, on unmet needs and on emergency feelings such as anger or resentment. These guidelines may help when you need to give such feedback.

- *Rarely give feedback to a person with low self-esteem.* An affirming relationship with this person would need to be established before he would be in a position not to perceive such feedback as threatening to self-esteem but to see it as purely an expression of something going on for the person giving the feedback.

- *Never give feedback in the presence of others.* This is a wise stipulation whether you are giving feedback, expressing reservations or asserting that a particular behaviour on the other person's part (principal, colleague, student) is not acceptable to you. It is best to do so privately and discreetly and always within the context of a valuing and respecting regard for the other person.

- *Raise the issue as soon as possible.* Delayed feedback on, for example, dissatisfaction or misgivings only leads to a build-up of tension within you and can lead later on to an out-of-proportion expression of the issue that was bothering you. Nevertheless, as indicated, timing and place of feed-back are all-important and these issues must be taken into consideration. The rule of thumb is to bring up your 'emergency' issue as soon as possible but in a place and at a time when it is least likely to create conflict between you and the other person.

- *Be clear and specific in your communication of your conflict.* Many people tend to be general in their expression of unmet needs and dissatisfactions. For example, for a teacher to say to a principal, 'I get no back-up or support in this school' is too general. What precisely is your need? Is it 'I need help and support to deal with student A from you as principal and from the other teachers who have this student in their classes'? This is much more specific; further questioning will clarify the conflict the teacher has with the particular student and what remedial actions are needed – on the part of the teacher himself, the principal and the other teachers, and the student.

- *Stick to the issue in hand.* Bringing into the discussion issues from the past escalates conflict. Going into the museum and pulling out all the old skeletons of the past which are not relevant to the issue in hand will only cloud the issue and, generally, cause more hurt, anger and confusion. Do not allow the other person or do not allow yourself to drift from the present-moment issue that you are concerned to talk out openly and to resolve. There is a technique called the 'broken record' which simply means repeating as often as is needed your feelings and unmet need on a particular issue. Taking up a previous example on not being consulted – 'John, when decisions are made on issues relating to my work and I haven't been consulted, I feel angry and I am asking that in future I be consulted on such matters' – if John replies 'I'm very busy, you know, lots of things on my mind', the appropriate response is 'I understand you're busy but when decisions are made . . . ' This process is repeated until you feel heard and a reasonable resolution has been reached.

- *Keep behaviour and person separate.* Do not confuse the behaviour which is a source of conflict for you with the person who is engaging in the behaviour. As indicated, what we typically do is label a person so that the person feels put down, judged and criticised. So, an insensitive remark becomes 'you're so insensitive', a child not making a responsible effort becomes 'you're lazy' or a principal who does not listen to a staff member's needs becomes 'he is impossible to talk to'. Labelling creates defensiveness and undermines the self-esteem of the receiver of your message. State specifically the 'bit' of behaviour that is causing difficulty for you and show how it blocks a particular need of yours.

- *Only use first-hand information.* Hearsay, reports from third parties, gossip and rumour are not desirable information sources on which to launch a confrontation on differences that you perceive as existing between you and a colleague. Refer to only first-hand experiences, situations in which you witnessed or directly experienced verbal or active opposition to values you hold dearly. In situations where a third party makes a complaint, be sure you remain impartial and listen to all sides.

- *Agree how to avoid repetitions.* When there is a serious difference between you and a colleague and one in which there is an agreement between you that the offence was a serious infringement of your rights or values, then some preventative mechanism needs to be decided upon. For example, if a colleague has berated you in front of other staff members, you might agree that in future differences would be communicated discreetly and on a one to one basis.

- *When the issue is resolved never bring it up again.* Try not to be like a dog with a bone – repeatedly gnawing on an issue that has been settled between you and a colleague. It is extremely punishing of another to frequently rake up past misdemeanours. Such behaviour may lead to serious mistrust on the part of the other. The past is something you learn from, not a stick to beat another with.

■ Affirmation of leaders

The guidelines regarding affirmations and bringing up 'difficult' issues apply not only to relationships between staff members but also to the relationship between staff and principals. Who affirms the leaders is an important issue. Very often staff are aware of their own needs for recognition and approval but forget that leaders have similar needs. Again, a cycle of staff–leader affirmation is likely to be reciprocated by leader–staff recognition and approval.

❏ *Problem-solving*

Within any social system problems arise. When such problems are not resolved the system is said to be dysfunctional, whereas when problems are responded to as challenges to improve relationships and resources within the troubled system, and are resolved, the system is said to be functional. What is interesting is that healthy systems – be they family, classroom, school, staff or community associations – appear to go through a step-by-step process of problem-solving, whereas dysfunctional systems may not even get to the first step of problem-solving which is identification of the problem. There are different problem-solving methods: the one suggested below is a seven-step method.

1. Identification of the problem

It is useful to catalogue problems into *instrumental* and *affective*. Instrumental problems are connected with resources and responsibilities. Typical examples are overcrowded classrooms, lack of secretarial assistance, lack of teaching tools, curriculum issues, problems in assignment of classes. Affective problems embrace personal and interpersonal emotional and behavioural problems. Examples include a principal who is overdominating and controlling or passive and non-assertive; a teacher having classroom management problems; a teacher with a personal problem of anxiety, depression or dependency on alcohol; high absenteeism of a teacher or student; a student who is shy and withdrawn; a student who is aggressive and non-cooperative.

An important element of this first step in problem-solving is who identifies the problem. If a student identifies the problem, he may not be taken seriously and the teacher's judgment may be given more credence. If a parent identifies a problem – for example, a teacher who is critical and aggressive within a classroom – what frequently happens is that teachers become defensive and do not respond positively to the identified problem. Or, if a teacher identifies the problematic behaviour of a colleague, often that teacher may not pursue the issue or may report the matter to the principal, who may, in turn, drop the matter. What a pity! Everybody now loses out – the school, the teacher who is not coping, the teacher who identified the problem, the students and the principal who is not exercising his leadership role.

Instrumental problems are far more frequently identified within school and classroom systems than affective issues. These tend to be much more threatening to an individual's self-esteem and, consequently, tend to be denied, suppressed or projected onto others. Sometimes the high emotional responses shown to instrumental issues, for example assignment of classes and hours, mask deeper affective problems within staff such as rivalry, resentment of favouritism, threat of failure or anger at not being consulted.

The important factor to be alert to when a problem is identified, whether affective or instrumental, is the emotional 'loading' that surrounds the problem; this is primarily identifiable in the non-verbal behaviours of the people concerned. Examples of these non-verbal signs are facial expression, tone of voice, loudness of voice, nervous mannerisms, lack of eye contact and body posture. Try to get to the feelings behind people's responses as this reveals the seriousness of the issue for them.

2. Communication of the problem

It is quite amazing what can happen at this stage of problem-solving. Very often nothing happens. The person who has identified the problem says nothing to anybody. Many students never reveal, to the principal, other teachers or their parents, victimisation by a particular teacher or group of peers. Similarly, there are teachers who are aware that a colleague is having serious difficulties within the classroom or is very fearful of a principal but do nothing about it. Typical outcomes that develop following problem identification are gossip or complaining, resignation that nothing can be done and blaming – none of which is constructive. It is important when a problem is identified that it is communicated to a source who can either advise what can be done or respond directly to the problem issues. Remember everybody benefits when a problem is positively responded to, and the problem is not an indictment of another person but an opportunity for growth within a system.

3. Brainstorming solutions to the problem

This is the most creative and dynamic step in the problem-solving process. It is where everybody concerned with the problem looks for solutions, the idea being to suggest any notion that comes into your head that might resolve the problem. It is important that all the individuals whom the problem affects be involved. Unfortunately, in many schools students are often not included in this process even though its outcome may directly affect them. A teacher having problems of management within a particular classroom would be wise to include all the members of that class in the brainstorming session. Sometimes parents may need to be invited in to give their suggestions for change. An essential aspect of brainstorming is that there must be no judging or criticism of proffered solutions no matter how ridiculous you may feel they are. Any judgments during brainstorming will quickly dry up creativity as people are not willing to risk the humiliation of being ridiculed. It is easy to see how a verbal judgment such as 'That's a load of rubbish' would sabotage brainstorming but much more subtle non-verbal messages like sighing, 'tut-tutting', a smile at another across the room or the raising of eyebrows can be equally devastating. All solutions must be written down and efforts continually affirmed.

4. Selection of an option

This can be the most difficult step as differences between problem-solvers are much more likely to appear at this point. It is always difficult to choose a solution that will suit everybody, and so, very often, a stalemate can come about. There are two issues here which, if considered together, make it less likely that entrenched positions will develop: one is the instrumental factor – what has to be done?; and the second is the affective or relationship factor – who will benefit from a commitment to a proposed solution? If only the 'what' is considered, people can be resistant to taking on more responsibilities but when relationships are also considered people tend to be more amenable to adopting a solution. For example, I may not be having any difficulty with classroom management and I am not enamoured of a proposed alternative management system which is going to make some demands on me. At an instrumental level the proposed option does not appeal but when I consider that it may greatly help a troubled colleague and students who may be exploiting a teacher's vulnerabilities, I am much more likely to commit myself to the solution. If I do not, I seriously need to ask myself: 'What is blocking me from helping a colleague or student who is in obvious distress?'

5. Action

This is the most important step as all the words in the world do not change situations but actions can and do. Sometimes, in spite of going through all the previous steps, nothing happens or only half-hearted efforts are made or commendable efforts are made but peter out after a short time. An insurance against the last outcome is an accountability system. Accountability is not a policing system but a method of ensuring the continuance of action through feedback, encouragement and support. The idea is that responsibilities are divided out among the members of a problem-solving group; then individuals or groups of individuals meet at set times and places to report to each other on progress and on any difficulties that may have arisen. For example, if four groups are formed then A reports to B, B to C, C to D, D to A. This accountability system must be well organised and executed.

6. Monitor progress of action

Is the execution of the option chosen having any effect? Let us assume that participants are truly trying but only a little change is occurring. It may well be that more or different action is needed so that a return to step 4 is needed for the selection of yet another option. If, on implementation of this added option, nothing much changes, the wrong problem or only a surface problem which was masking a deeper issue may have been identified. A return to step 1 will be required in order to identify the real problem. As already pointed out, very often instrumental issues mask deeper affective issues. For example, where two or three schools in a local area amalgamate, subsequent conflict on instrumental issues, on deeper investigation, can reveal hidden fears of one group not feeling valued by the other staff members of what was the more desirable school in the local area. Similar affective difficulties may arise when an all-male school staff joins an all-female school staff. Another affective issue is where teachers of the so-called 'less important' subjects like religion, domestic science and civics feel less recognised and valued in the school system. Indeed, subjects like religion and civics have become the hardest to teach because they are not examination courses, and consequently motivation to listen and learn is not high among students. I know of many religion and civics teachers who have management problems in classrooms. Also, Irish has become a difficult subject to teach because of poor motivation and its relevance not being appreciated. All these difficulties need to be recognised within a school system and corrective actions taken with the support of all staff.

7. Evaluation of problem-solving strategy

The main purpose of this step is to evaluate the strategy used in the present problem-solving situation so that lessons can be learnt and applied in the resolution of other issues which will inevitably arise in the future. Problems will never be totally eliminated from the educational system. New problems will arise in response to changing economic, social, moral, religious, political and psychological circumstances within the wider society. These problems are challenges to the educational system to respond to the different needs that have emerged in the population of students, teachers, managers, parents and employers who either directly or indirectly use the system. Previous experience of conflict-resolution can aid the resolution of difficulties in the future when the insights and effective strategies gained are brought to bear on the new problem/challenge. Beware though of assuming that what worked before will automatically work again.

❏ *Responding to rigidity in self and others*

A difficult aspect of the development of healthy staff relationships is coping with a principal or colleague who is inflexible
and rigid in his behaviour. People with such problematic behaviour live their lives according to numerous laws of 'shoulds',
'should nots', 'have tos', 'musts' and 'ought tos'. One of the
very few times Christ got angry in the Gospels was when he
said to the Pharisees: 'You make it as if man is made for the
law but man is greater than the law and the law is there for
man to use wisely and compassionately'. At another time,
Christ said: 'All laws are put aside; all man needs to do is love
God with all his heart and love his neighbour as himself'.
Indeed, the love of self was the best-kept secret in the Catholic
Church. How wise of Christ to see that when man truly values
himself, others and his universe, there is no need for laws.
The problem in many countries, and many social systems, is
that people do not respect and value each other. When that is
the case laws, rules and regulations evolve as protectors
against neglect, abuse, exploitation and rejection.

To be able to cope and respond effectively to the person
exhibiting a rigid approach demands an in-depth understanding of the nature and function of rigidity. A case-study will
help to clarify this issue. This was a young science teacher, in
his late twenties, who was referred to me with high blood
pressure and stomach ulcers – serious signs of stress. The
nature of his rigidity was that he had to be the 'perfect'
teacher. He spent hours preparing classes because he had to
know everything and to be able to answer any questions from
students in the classroom. He spent the entire school day
writing work for the students on the blackboard – leaving no
room for mistakes or control difficulties in the classroom!
Any extracurricular activities that needed to be done in the
school he would volunteer to do, and he would do them
perfectly. Quite innocently he boasted to me that since he had
taken over the St Vincent de Paul Fund in the school he had
collected more money than anyone before him. You might say
what a prize this man was for the school. However, the effects
on him were life-threatening and, no doubt, he was projecting
his own irrational standards onto students, thereby putting

them under pressure. Before he went to school each morning, he literally used to get sick with the dread and worry about the day: 'Will I manage? will I remember everything I've prepared? will I be able to control the class? will I be approved by colleagues and principal?' These high anxieties pushed up his blood pressure and 'knotted' his stomach. Of course, he let nobody see these vulnerabilities. Though sick he would never be absent. In all his eight years of teaching he had never missed a day.

Now all human behaviour has a function but what possibly could be the purpose of such rigidity and inflexibility? The answer is protection. His rigidity is a protection against multiple fears of failure, criticism and rejection. How clever to develop rigid attitudes of perfectionism such as 'If I'm perfect in all that I do, how can I then experience failure, criticism or rejection?' Indeed, how could you? – except that it is impossible to be perfect in behaviour at all times and hence the anxiety that his defence behaviours might not be strong enough. Nonetheless, the strategy works most of the time. But why is this young man, very intellectually able, living life in constant fear and rigidity? Fears arise from dependency. Clearly he is very dependent on approval and acceptance from others and on success. But take it a step deeper, why is he so dependent? The answer to this is that he has little regard for himself, deeply doubts his capabilities – in short, he had low self-esteem. And one more step, whence the low self-esteem? Low self-esteem, as you have seen, comes from unresolved conflicts in childhood. No matter how well he did as a child, whether it was academically, athletically or otherwise, the response from both his parents was 'Well, you could have done better'.

The clear message he got in these early years of his life was 'You are never good enough'. What a sad legacy to give a child! He now develops no inner conviction of his own worthiness, and remains dependent and fearful of other people's judgments. Now we see the wisdom of the rigid attitudes; it is as if he is saying to his parents: 'If I'm perfect will you love and approve of me?' Rigid behaviours are always protectors – weapons against hurt and rejection. To try to take away a person's rigidity without understanding its purpose will always fail. People who are rigid in attitudes and behaviour become even more so when confronted, the reason being that they are afraid of losing the weapon that protects them. The problem is that the weapon puts psychological and physical health at risk.

As can be seen below, rigidity masks emotional problems and so the response to the person displaying rigid cognitive and behavioural patterns must be at the emotional levels. To move in at the cognitive or behavioural levels would risk losing contact with the person, as these levels are protectors of low self-esteem and therefore will only weaken when self-esteem is elevated. When self-esteem rises, dependency and fears reduce and the need for protectors in the form of rigidities disappears. The staff member or student who is regarded as 'rigid' and 'impossible' needs affirmation, affection, encouragement, support and, most of all, belief in their worthiness in terms of their lovability and capability. In short, the person needs to be unconditionally valued.

Physical	**Psychosomatic complaints** (heart disease, blood pressure, stomach problems, headaches) $\updownarrow$
Behavioural	**Rigid behaviours** (overworking, imbalanced lifestyle, not listening to feedback, authoritarianism, passive-manipulation) $\updownarrow$
Cognitive	**Rigid attitudes** ('people should accept me', 'I should be perfect in what I do', 'I shouldn't fail') $\updownarrow$
Emotional	**Fears of rejection, disapproval, criticism, failure** $\updownarrow$
Emotional	**Dependency** ('I need to be valued and approved by parents/others') $\updownarrow$
Emotional	**Low self-esteem** ('I am not good enough for my parents/others') $\updownarrow$
Emotional	**Unresolved childhood conflicts** (conditionality or total neglect)

Any system where a person or different groups of people do not value each other gives rise to rigid 'protective' patterns of behaviour. It is incumbent on all members of such a system to create a social and emotional environment where members will not have to protect themselves from disrespect, hurt and rejection but rather feel safe and secure in the evident value that each member shows to the other.

❑ *Key insights*

- Staff relationships are a major source of stress within the school system.
- It is of significance to all members of staff when a colleague has a self-esteem problem.
- Protective, unsupportive patterns of communication are the most common forms of relating in staffrooms.
- Open/relating patterns of communication create a supportive and positive school environment where teachers can feel safe in voicing their difficulties and getting help and support for them.
- Many conflicts on instrumental issues mask deeper affective conflicts.
- Communication is primarily about revealing and getting one's needs met. Many needs are not met because of dysfunctional communication.
- Vulnerability and weaknesses are strengths.
- There are welfare feelings and emergency feelings and both are positive.
- Never asking for help is an act of dependence.
- Staff morale is the lifeblood of a school's staff group.
- Problem-solving approaches are an inherent part of effective social systems.
- Rigidity is a symptom of emotional insecurity.

❑ *Key actions*

- Develop open/relating patterns of communication which are: non-judgmental, permissive, spontaneous, empathic, egalitarian and provisional.

- Send an 'I' message that is direct and clear when expressing any need.
- Express all your feelings in full openness.
- Be independent by seeking help and support when you need it and allowing the receiver freedom to say 'yes' or 'no'.
- Create positive staff morale through:
  - high level of staff interaction
  - group decision-making
  - leader availability and approachability
  - leader and staff affirmation of staff
  - staff affirmation of leaders
  - constructive communication of differences, unmet needs and emergency feelings.
- Develop an effective problem-solving approach to conflict issues.
- Show affirmation, affection, recognition, support, encouragement and belief in their worthiness to staff members or students who display rigidity.

CHAPTER 4

The Student

❑ *Maladaptive behaviour is always right*
❑ *Signs of students' emotional conflicts*
❑ *Teacher–student relationships*
  ▪ Absence of relationship
  ▪ Relationship devoid of feelings
  ▪ Narcissistic relationship
  ▪ Overinvolved relationship
  ▪ Symbiotic relationship
  ▪ Empathic relationship
❑ *Student self-esteem in the classroom*
  ▪ Identifying students with low self-esteem
  ▪ Self-esteem and learning
  ▪ Increasing self-esteem in the classroom
    ↝ **Self-esteem-enhancing messages**
    ↝ **Self-esteem-enhancing actions**
❑ *Key insights*
❑ *Key actions*

❑ *Maladaptive behaviour is always right*

Students presenting with behavioural difficulties within schools have become a major source of stress in teaching. In most cases an authoritarian response to these students no longer works and neither is it desirable. Authoritarianism dehumanises and blocks the mature development of children. Yet many schools and individual teachers have not discovered constructive approaches to disruptive behaviours. A full understanding of the nature of pupils' maladaptive behaviours can lead to the development of appropriate responses to them.

The first insight that is needed is that students' maladaptive behaviour is always right. Sounds like a paradox, does it not? How could behaviour like fidgeting, inattentiveness, aggressive outbursts, insolence, refusals to do work, temper tantrums and so on be right? They are right because they are symptoms or signs of underlying conflicts within the child: they are not the problem but revelations or manifestations of it. Unfortunately, because these behavioural manifestations disrupt teaching they become problems to teachers and indeed to other students. The reaction is to punish them. However, in spite of the punishments, the behaviours tend to persist, because the core of the problem has not been identified and the punishing response only aggravates that unidentified problem.

Let us take an example. I remember being invited into a primary school in England to deal with a child who was causing serious behavioural difficulties within the classroom. I got to the school before classes started and the child was pointed out to me by his class teacher as he filed past us into the classroom. He was displaying no maladaptive behaviours at that moment. I noticed that this seven-year-old child was quite small and thin for his age, somewhat pale and emaciated, with clothing dishevelled. As he passed me by there was a strong smell of urine from the child. I had agreed with the principal and class teacher that I would sit at the back of the class and observe this child. Once children get into classroom they tend to forget about the existence of an observer. The child, let us call him Mark, went to his desk, took his books out of his bag and put them into his desk. When the class was requested to take out a particular book he duly complied. For about fifteen minutes the child cooperated with the teaching demands but then, very audibly, began to make noises with the flap of his desk. Immediately the teacher came down to him and said: 'Stop that noise Mark'. A few minutes later when her attention was off him he pulled at the student in front of him. Once again the teacher came down to him and corrected him. This cycle of maladaptive behaviours and the teacher's correction of them continued for the rest of the class up to the eleven o'clock break. The teacher spent much of her class time correcting Mark's disruptive behaviour. However, her ridiculing and scolding were having little or no impact.

Surely you will say that the teacher had to do what she was doing? My point is that no understanding of the child's maladaptive behaviour was present in her response to its appearance. I had already guessed what the deeper issue was. I enquired from the principal and class teacher about the home circumstances of the child. It transpired he was from a broken home. His father had left three years before and had maintained no contact with the family; his mother was under considerable stress, working in a factory, and very impatient and irritable with her son. She was gone to work before he left for school and the child was not being fed in the mornings; neither was he being washed. I also discovered he was a bedwetter. After school the child often had to sit outside his home for a number of hours before his mother came home. I explained to the class teacher and principal that the child's maladaptive behaviours were a sign of underlying conflict of not feeling wanted and that he had a massive unmet need to be seen and loved. I also pointed out that unless these underlying needs were met in the classroom it was unlikely that progress would be made in reducing his disruptive behaviours. I further illustrated that the disruptive behaviours were gaining him some attention but that when he engaged in responsible behaviours no response was given. I suggested that the response the child needed was for his class teacher to develop an affirming, valuing and close relationship with him. This would meet his unmet needs and reduce his conflict of not feeling wanted. I also stressed that when the child engaged in responsible behaviours these should get immediate reinforcing responses from the teacher. This would lead to an increase in responsible actions and a corresponding decrease in the disruptive ones. I also advised that the disruptive actions should be ignored as much as possible and when this was not possible, should be corrected in a firm but positive manner.

The class teacher quickly saw how she had been unwittingly increasing the child's maladaptive behaviours and she also saw the wisdom of attending to the child's responsible behaviours. She adopted this policy and there was a considerable improvement in the child's behaviour within the classroom. The teacher resisted the notion of the need for a close relationship with the child. Her response to this request was: 'I treat all the children in the classroom in the same way'. I said that would be fine if all the children were the same but that this child needed help because of his unfortunate circumstances.

She confessed she could not warm to him. I also arranged help for the mother and, with her agreement, had the child washed and fed when he came to school. The principal also agreed to give more attention to him. The following September, the child entered a new class and the new teacher established a very warm affirming relationship with him. Interestingly, he manifested no difficulties during his year with her.

So, maladaptive behaviours are 'right' because they manifest the inner conflicts of children. Nevertheless, the same behaviours are also 'unacceptable' because they disrupt classes and schools and because they are not desirable or adaptive ways of getting needs met. However, it is important to realise that the child is not deliberately engaging in these behaviours but knows of no other way to get his needs met. More than likely adaptive ways did not work in the home for the child and, in desperation, the maladaptive ways developed as a last resort. More importantly, the maladaptive behaviours are signs and these must not be shown in vain by the child. What is also important is that the underlying issue is different for each child so that there is no general way of responding to an individual child's conflict. What I have learned in helping children, adolescents and adults over the years is that each person who comes to me for help needs a different therapy.

Why do we refer to children's disruptive behaviours as maladaptive? Take a child who is very clinging so that he goes around pulling on his mother's skirt all day. In what way is the behaviour maladaptive? It is maladaptive because it never resolves the child's underlying conflict and, indeed, often exacerbates it. When a child constantly clings, very often the parent will get irritated and push the child away with a scolding remark such as 'Stop pulling out of me'. Such a response plunges the child back into his frightening conviction that he is not loved and so the conflict increases. Similarly, children who steal very often are manifesting hurt and anger because many of their rights to be loved, cared for, nurtured, protected, given freedom and challenged were stolen from them by parents who either badly neglected or overcontrolled and dominated them. Unfortunately, the stealing results in further condemnation by parents and so the hidden conflict remains.

The understanding of students' maladaptive behaviours can be illustrated as follows:

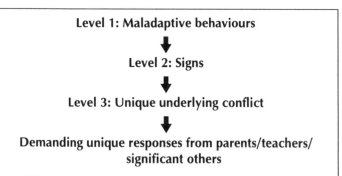

Level 1: Maladaptive behaviours
↓
Level 2: Signs
↓
Level 3: Unique underlying conflict
↓
Demanding unique responses from parents/teachers/ significant others

The response of parents, teachers and other significant adults to the child's conflicts must occur at all levels; focusing on level 1 without identifying or responding to level 3 is unlikely to be successful. The rest of this chapter suggests ways of responding at level 3; Chapter 5 concentrates on level 1.

❏ *Signs of students' emotional conflicts*

The signs of emotional conflict among children may be categorised under three main headings: physical, undercontrol and overcontrol signs. The physical signs are common to those students who manifest problematic responses under either of the other two categories. Signs of undercontrol are those behaviours that can be very troublesome to others but are, nonetheless, clear signs of emotional disturbance. The student acts out his inner conflicts in a subconscious attempt to get his needs met. Typical undercontrol behaviours are aggressiveness, insolence, bullying and hyperactivity. Psychologically these behaviours are saying something 'right' about the student but socially the behaviours can make it very difficult to teach a class or manage a school. Because these undercontrol behaviours are socially unacceptable, some action is needed to either reduce or extinguish their occurrence. However, this must only be done in the context of an attempt to discover the psychological 'rightness' of these upsetting manifestations. It is interesting, and also understandable, that children who exhibit undercontrol behaviours are most likely to be referred to principals, school counsellors and back-up psychological and social services. It is also of note that boys are more likely than girls to manifest their inner conflicts through undercontrol behaviours.

More girls than boys engage in overcontrol behaviours but many boys do so also. These behaviours also are a subconscious effort to have emotional problems seen. Overcontrol problem behaviours, such as shyness, overdiligence and perfectionism do not in any serious way upset the classroom or school. The quiet, withdrawn child does not interfere with classroom work; this child usually is not seen as problematic and therefore does not get the help he needs. Unfortunately, he is often more at risk than his peers who 'act out' their problems. It is as if those who shout the loudest are more likely to be heard. It is important therefore that teachers be vigilant for overcontrol signs of emotional conflict. The signs of undercontrol do not need such vigilance as they will very strongly wake you up to the presence of students who have unmet emotional needs.

The hope is that both sets of children will have their needs detected and appropriately responded to, and that more adaptive ways of getting their needs met will be taught to them. There is no doubt that teachers are becoming more aware of and more concerned about the emotional and social welfare of their students, and want to learn how to create a healthy emotional climate within the classroom and school.

It is not difficult for teachers to identify the at-risk child. There are multiple manifestations of the unmet needs of children. When such behavioural manifestations are regularly shown, appropriate and constructive responses are needed in the classroom and school with back-up from the family. Typical signs of distress within classroom or school settings are outlined below. A student who is regularly showing two or more of these behaviours is manifesting clear signs of emotional conflict.

Typical signs of students' inner conflicts

Physical signs

Nail biting • facial grimacing • restlessness • stammering • sudden blushing or paling • frequent twitching of muscles • poor physical coordination • bedwetting • soiling • frequent complaints of headaches • stomach aches or other pains • obesity • loss of weight • poor appetite • jumping at sudden noises • loss of energy • affectations or posturings

Signs of undercontrol

Personal signs: student

Behaviour too young for age • hyperactivity • irresponsible behaviour • impulsiveness • little academic effort • mischievousness • inability to work alone • overexcitable • uncontrolled laughing or giggling • high distractibility • extravagant emotional expression • frequent nightmares • speaking too fast • destructiveness of school property • defacing of books • abusive or obscene language • writing obscenities on walls • lying • cheating • thieving • hatred of school work • does not learn from experience • favours out-of-class activities • blaming of others for mistakes and failures • highly critical of others • show-off • truanting from school

Interpersonal signs: teacher

Frequent requests for help • attention-seeking • crushes on teachers • effort to curry favour with teachers • staying persistently after class to talk with teacher • frequently disruptive in class • many requests for special attentions and favours • irrelevant answers to questions • acting tough in class • exaggerated courtesy • constant bragging • inability to take criticism • frequent justification of self • misinterpretation of what teachers say • false accusations of teachers • frequent complaints of unfair treatment • complaints that teachers or parents 'have it in' for him • extreme suspiciousness of teachers' motives • insolence • temper or aggressive outbursts when corrected or requested to do something • resentment of authority • unwillingness to obey rules and regulations • hostile reactions to discipline

Interpersonal signs: other students

Bullying • teasing • pushiness • trying to be funny • acting tough • dominating and controlling younger or smaller students • showing off • abusive or obscene language • frequent verbal and physical 'fights' with peers • regular complaints that other students do not like him • frequent relaying of 'dirty' stories • overinterest in sexual matters

Signs of overcontrol

Personal signs: student

Extreme shyness • poor or no self-confidence • strong tendency to remain alone • homesickness • school 'phobia' • highly insecure and anxious • timidity • fearfulness of new situations • mutism • avoidance of school games • tendency to stay apart at break times • excessive academic efforts • frequent daydreaming • worries unduly • frequently looks sad • poor motivation to learn • appears 'lost in another world' • obsessional and/or compulsive behaviours • overexact • meticulous • undue anxiety over performance • undue distress over mistakes and failures • preoccupation with scholastic results • 'perfect' student

Interpersonal signs: teacher

Poor response to recognition and praise • irrelevant answers to questions • failure to respond when addressed • poor or no spontaneous participation in class • overattachment to one teacher • little or no contact with teachers • no requests for help • hypersensitive to criticism • feelings easily hurt • no eye contact • extreme nervousness when answering questions • frequent breaking off of speech in the middle of a sentence • frequent mental blocks when either answering questions or doing an examination

Interpersonal signs: other students

Few or no friends • overt rejection by peers • avoidance of students of opposite sex • absence from school events • avoidance of team games • frequent target of fun by other students

As already mentioned, each student's conflict is peculiar to his home and school circumstances and has to be understood and responded to within those special contexts. Nevertheless, we know that all children or adolescents who manifest problems within school inevitably have self-esteem problems. Research has also shown that many learning difficulties are related to low self-esteem and so the primary target of remedial teachers needs to be the elevation of the child's self-esteem. When this is accomplished the child becomes motivated and open to academic input. It has already been pointed out that teachers who establish close affirming relationships with pupils are the most effective teachers because affirming relationships of their very nature elevate the self-esteem of students. One of the primary means of raising students' self-esteem is through the relationship that teachers have with students in the classroom. The type of relationship will determine whether or not self-esteem is positively affected. Whether teachers are aware of it or not, a student's self-esteem is constantly being affected by teachers' interactions with him.

❑ *Teacher–student relationships*

There are six types of teacher–student relationships that can operate within a school:

- absence of relationship
- relationship devoid of feelings
- narcissistic relationship
- overinvolved relationship
- symbiotic relationship
- empathic relationship.

Primary school children can be fortunate if they have an affirming, positive teacher as they will have that teacher for at least a year and sometimes longer. Of course the reverse is also true – primary school children can be stuck with a strict, critical, negative, punishing teacher for a considerable length of time. Matters are much more confusing for second-level pupils because in any one day they can experience a range of different types of relationships with the different teachers they encounter. Five of the six types of relationships described below damage self-esteem while one, empathic relationship, enhances it.

■ Absence of relationship

In this classroom a student may be totally ignored or dismissed by a teacher. Nothing that the student does will gain him recognition or approval from the teacher. It is literally a 'no-win' situation. A student in this classroom who has middle to low self-esteem will be seriously adversely affected by this teacher. A student with high self-esteem will also be minimally affected but generally will get support and help from home to withstand the negative effects of this relationship. The teacher who operates in this non-relating way has serious, deep-seated self-esteem difficulties and needs professional help.

■ Relationship devoid of feelings

This teacher–student relationship is purely clinical or instrumental in nature. The teacher shows no warmth or closeness to students. She is there to teach and not to relate. As in the last type of relationship this is a 'no-win' situation. There is nothing that the student can do to gain approval or acceptance from this teacher. Very often this teacher is seen as a 'good' teacher as she will prepare her classes well and deliver academic material effectively within the classroom. However, her action will have no elevating effect on self-esteem and for those students with middle to low self-esteem, her 'cold' relating can have a devastating effect. This teacher also has an enormous self-esteem problem.

■ Narcissistic relationship

The narcissistic teacher–student relationship is a conditional relationship where the pupil can gain recognition and affirmation but at a cost. In effect, the teacher is saying to the student 'you are there for me'. In this relationship the student is there to meet the teacher's needs and when he does so he will gain praise and approval. This teacher is dependent on her own professional performance as a means of gaining approval from others and acceptance of self. Once the students measure up to this teacher's standards they will be affirmed and praised. However, if they fall short they are then likely to be dismissed, ignored, criticised, compared to the students who are measuring up, ridiculed and scolded. All of these responses damage students' self-esteem and perpetuate the dependency and self-esteem difficulties of the teacher. The sad thing is that the children who 'fall short' of the teacher's unrealistic demands are those who already will have middle to low self-esteem: exposure to such a narcissistic relationship will further lower their feelings about themselves. It is important to see that most parents and teachers are narcissistic in behaviour to some degree. This is manifested in the conditional way that most children are reared. As we have already seen, typical conditions that operate in many homes and classrooms are: be good, behave, be clever, be like me, be quick, be unquestioning, be perfect, be athletic. The withdrawal of affection and affirmation from children breaking these conditions is what leads to self-esteem difficulties. Behaviour now becomes the measure of the child's worth, and love is the weapon used to shape the child's development.

▪ Overinvolved relationship

This is also a conditional relationship but opposite in nature to narcissistic relating. The basis for this type of relationship is again the need for acceptance and approval arising from a teacher's poor self-esteem. This teacher is the 'people-pleaser': she goes to extremes in order to be 'needed' by students and colleagues. This teacher feels that she cannot be done without, and works long hours and takes on extracurricular activities as a means of developing this indispensability. Remember these actions are subconsciously motivated, and any confrontation on their 'martyrdom' nature will evoke such defensive responses as 'my job is all-important to me', 'people need me' and so on. Compared to narcissistic relationships this overinvolved interacting says 'I am there for you' and 'as long as you let me do things for you and be a part of your life, I will accept and value you'. The real, but hidden, issue is 'I can't live without someone needing or approving of me'. The condition for acceptance is quite clear: 'need me'. Students who do not respond to this condition and who want to be independent in decision-making and in ways of doing things and who generally want to be separate and not overprotected will be rejected by this teacher, mainly in the form of withdrawal, silence and even sulking.

So, both narcissistic relating and overinvolved relating mask similar self-esteem problems. The former employs dominance and control to gain recognition, while the latter uses 'people-pleasing'. Either way the student clearly loses out if he does not respond. But even if he does meet the conditions, he still suffers in the long run on two accounts: he develops a dependency on the teacher for approval, and he sacrifices his own identity formation and independence in order to please the teacher.

■ Symbiotic relationship

This is a very disturbing relationship where no individuality is allowed and each member of the class must be the same in all aspects of behaviour. It is as if the class is the individual and the members make up that one body. This used to be very common in monasteries and convents. I spent seven years in a semi-enclosed order myself and during those years we had to dress the same, have the same philosophical and theological ideas, walk the same, eat the same food and so on. Individuality and independence were anathema. Any attempt to be different was severely punished. Some classrooms and staffrooms can be symbiotic, where the teacher or principal demands this sameness and absolute interdependency. Because this style of relating attempts to totally block identity development and independence, which are the bases of high self-esteem, it is extremely damaging. In fact its effects are as great as for absence of relationship and relationship devoid of feelings.

These five ways of relating increase insecurity and lack of confidence and lower self-esteem in children. Each student needs the teacher–student relationship to demonstrate that his presence is valuable and worthwhile within each class and within the school. It is equally important that a student's absence matters and that this is communicated to him. Many teachers 'breathe a sigh of relief' when a particular pupil is absent and when that student returns the non-verbal language will be one that reveals 'oh no, he's back!' Children are excellent at reading non-verbal behaviour and when this is negative their sense of value is undermined. It is necessary then that the student feels that both his presence and absence matter.

▪ Empathic relationship

Fortunately, there is a healthy, self-esteem-building way for teachers to interact with students. This type of relationship is of an unconditional nature where each student is valued and affirmed for his unique person and being. Students' differences in size, shape, colour, social background, level of knowledge and academic or athletic skills are respected and appreciated. Teachers show interest in each student because they value and respect him as a unique human being deserving of affirmation. In this unconditional interaction the valuing relationship is seen as the priority and is never broken because of unacceptable behaviours, mistakes or failures. The affirmative teacher is just as strict as the conditional, rigid and authoritarian teacher when it comes to children learning to take responsibility for their actions. But this firmness is executed always within the context of the warm and affirming relationship. Furthermore, the child is not 'put down' but is helped to become aware of the necessity to learn responsibility; if he attempts to slide out of responsibility the teacher has no choice but to impose consequences. Criticism, scoldings, 'put-down' messages, ridicule, comparing students, sarcasm and cynicism are absent in this teacher–student relationship. Furthermore, the child is encouraged to express in constructive ways his opinions and any worries, fears, grievances, resentments, frustration or difficulties he may be experiencing. At all times the child knows that he is accepted for his person and that behaviour is not the yardstick to measure worth.

❏ *Student self-esteem in the classroom*

As you have seen, the hidden conflicts of children presenting problems within the classroom are virtually always related to self-esteem. It is then in the interest of the class teacher and all other teachers in the school to find ways of elevating the feelings and attitudes these students possess about themselves. Elevation of student self-esteem will considerably decrease the amount and intensity of classroom problems.

■ Identifying students with low self-esteem

Identifying the student with poor self-esteem is not difficult and the short checklist below should help.

Checklist for low self-esteem in students	
Overcontrol indicators	**Undercontrol indicators**
• Shy and withdrawn	• Boastful
• Reluctant to take on new activities/challenges	• Regular truant
• Unable to mix easily with other students	• Frequent requester of help or reassurance
• Overconscientious or apathetic in learning situations	• Attention-seeking
• Fearful and timid in new situations	• Continually asking if he is liked or popular
• Easily upset if corrected	• Avoider of work even though risking teacher's disapproval
• Day-dreamer	• Blaming of others for own mistakes or failures
• Fearful of failures and mistakes	• Prone to regular aggressive outbursts
• In the habit of putting self down	

■ Self-esteem and learning

Teachers are often puzzled by students who clearly possess the skills to learn but make no effort. The high self-esteem child will have retained a natural curiosity for learning and will be enthusiastic when presented with a new challenge. This child is confident in social situations and in tackling academic assignments. But the middle to low self-esteem child has lost that excitement of learning; indeed any learning means risking failure and mistakes, and these have only brought humiliation and rejection in the past. It is safer to risk a teacher's disapproval than the embarrassment and punishment of failure.

Success and failure in themselves have no effect on a child's motivation to learn but the reactions of parents, teachers and other significant adults to success and failure can have a devastating effect. When adults react positively to successful performances and punishingly to failure, a child begins to doubt both his ability to please and his capability. The child then has to find ways of protecting himself from such harsh conditionality. There are, in effect, two choices open to him: *avoidance* or *compensation*. Both of these subconscious reactions are survival strategies for living in a painful world of conditionality. The more extreme the reactions of significant adults, the more intense and enduring will be the child's protective behaviours.

Avoidance of scholastic demands is such a clever strategy because it means that with no effort there can be no failure, and no failure means no humiliation. Unfortunately, a teacher may become frustrated, annoyed and angry with an avoidant student and blame, ridicule or scold him. This will drive the child further into the conviction that he is worthless in the eyes of adults, and his avoidance behaviour will increase in spite of the punishment meted out.

The second survival strategy is compensation. This can take two forms: the child either fights back at the source of frustration or tries extremely hard to please both parents and teachers. The latter is very often seen as virtuous by adults but teachers need to be vigilant in noticing this child because failure and mistakes, or even a small drop in standard of performance, can be a devastating blow to this child's sense of self. These overintense students tend to have a higher risk of suicide and can experience severe anxiety and panic attacks coming up to examination time. Sometimes they may be hospitalised and have often been misclassified as suffering from 'schizophrenia'.

It reminds me of an A-level student in England who was referred to me for psychotherapy. She had been one of the best students the school ever had. She was extremely attentive in class, no absenteeism, conscientious in completing home-work assignments, A-level performance in all subjects – the perfect student! When she went into her A-level year in September the teachers began to notice a radical change in her classroom behaviour. For the first time she was clearly not listening and she began to fail to complete assignments. They also noticed that she seemed quite distressed; this manifested itself in facial grimacing. At home she spent all her time locked away in her bedroom. She was unwilling to talk to anyone about what was disturbing her. Finally, after three weeks her mother persuaded her to reveal her conflict. The girl was terrified because she felt, in her own words, that she was 'possessed by the devil'. She was brought to a psychiatrist who labelled her 'schizo-phrenic' and had her hospitalised and put on medication. Her parents were dissatisfied with her progress and had heard from a teacher within the school that I worked in a non-organic way with people labelled 'schizophrenic'. On discharge from hospital, the girl came to see me with her parents.

The school had already contacted me and I had developed some insights into her ways of behaving and the high academic performance pressures on the girl from teachers, parents and herself. The school principal had outlined her 'brilliant' academic record and the fact that the girl was a very quiet and reserved person never giving any trouble. When I went to my waiting room she was sitting between her parents, clearly in a highly stressed state. All her features were distorted, her head was bowed and her body twisting as in agony. I was worried that she might be too disassociated from reality and not be able to respond to my helping efforts. I invited her on her own over to my office. I had already asked myself the question 'why now?' This girl seemed to have coped well up to the September of this year but had suffered a radical change in behaviour since returning to school. Clearly, being her last year in secondary school, her A-levels year, the pressure on her to perform would be greater than it ever had been before. So the difference was that this was her A-levels year. The fact that this girl bottled up all her feelings and problems meant that her conflict would not reveal itself through conscious behaviours (what you say, think and feel) but through unconscious means. The language of the unconscious is metaphorical and, in my experience, delusions and hallucinations are messages regarding hidden conflicts. It is accepted that dreams reveal conflicts in our lives that need resolution. Hallucinations and delusions are like 'waking dreams', attempts by the psyche to wake people up to intrapsychic and extrapsychic issues that need to be changed in their lives. This girl had interpreted literally her feeling of being possessed by the devil and her reaction was one of terror that she was going insane. The psychiatrist interpreted that delusion as an organic dysfunction. But when you see the delusion as meaningful, the sense of it begins to emerge.

I knew this young person had attained a high level of knowledge and, if she was hearing me, she would begin to get insight into her crisis experience. I explained to her how the mind reveals conflicts in different ways, through aggression, withdrawal, hostility, negative thinking, dependency, fears and metaphor. I explained that I felt that her 'being possessed by the devil' was a clear message to her of the intense pressure she had been undergoing in this all-important examination year. I said: 'It seems to me that you have "a devil of a pressure" inside you, and that also, since the beginning of September, you have "gone to the devil" in not being attentive in class and completing assignments'. 'Furthermore', I explained, 'it would appear to me that all these people that have been putting pressure on you for high scholastic performance, that you would want to say to them "go to the devil".' As I outlined my hypotheses to this girl, her facial grimacing and body twisting began to ease, and at the end of the session she was quiet and relaxed. She now had meaning for her so-called 'insane' experiences.

I brought her parents in and explained to them what I felt was the problem. The father was quick to see my explanation and wisely responded by saying 'we're the ones that need the therapy'. He recognised the immense pressure they had been putting on their daughter. I asked both parents to go to the sidelines of their daughter's life and have no more talk about examinations and academic performance. I also contacted the school and asked teachers not to put pressure on the girl. The three of them, daughter and parents, came for therapy sessions over the following six months. The girl returned to school the day after her first session and the school reported an 80 per cent improvement in the first week. Following two more therapeutic sessions there was a 100 per cent return to attentiveness and completion of assignments. The following summer the girl attained remarkably high A-level results and went on to university. However, the overcompensation strategy had ceased: she no longer felt she had to prove herself to her parents, others and self, and realised she could enjoy learning for learning's sake.

The child then who tries too hard, who overemphasises school work and neglects social, emotional, creative, athletic and leisure activities, has low self-esteem and is attempting to compensate for this inner insecurity by being the best student. The rationale is: 'If I'm the best, will you now love me Mum, Dad and teacher?'

The other type of compensation is revealed in boastful, aggressive, 'chip on the shoulder' type behaviour. This is the student who rebels against those who impose high and unrealistic demands on him. The pose of this student is: 'I can do anything if I put my mind to it, but why should I please you, why should I bother?' The sad thing is that it bothers him greatly that he is not valued but he is not going to show that vulnerability to anyone. This student has developed yet another clever strategy to avoid failure and humiliation. His rebelliousness means he avoids having to apply himself to academic demands and therefore avoids any risk of failure. If you attempt to coerce him into applying himself to his studies he will resist all the more and may act out quite violently. By pushing him you are getting too close to his vulnerability, his fear of failure and rejection, and so he now has to defend himself more fiercely.

It can be seen that all three types of defence strategies employed by students with low self-esteem have the common element of an attempt to avoid failure and humiliation. The overintense student avoids failure through high work input, the student who is arrogant and boastful avoids failure through non-compliance, and the student who is withdrawn and apathetic avoids failure through absence of effort. Why? Because there is a prime need in our culture for self-regard: a need to be liked and valued.

An important rule for both parents and teachers to be aware of is that while unrealistic demands lead to low self-esteem, equally no demands at all lead to low self-esteem because no belief is shown in the child's capability. In both cases children are doomed to low achievement or overachievement. Effective parents and teachers know that there is an optimum pressure – just enough to cause the child to feel challenged and positive but not so much that he becomes distressed. The secret is to be aware of the child's present level of functioning and to work out from there in a realistic manner.

Without attention to self-esteem students are not likely to make long-term academic progress. Research is showing that, in general, people's levels of achievement are influenced by how they see themselves and, more specifically, that self-esteem and scholastic achievement are strongly associated. A teacher in the classroom is in a powerful position to influence how students feel about themselves. The most important vehicle the teacher has is the relationship with the students, and when this is valuing and caring in nature students' self-esteem will be elevated. Teaching then is more effective when teachers concentrate both on the development of scholastic abilities and on the student's affective state, particularly self-esteem. Education is not just about developing intellectual and occupational skills, it is also about helping students to understand and value themselves, to be able to communicate in effective ways with others, to appreciate and celebrate all aspects of life, to develop healthy relationships with others and their world, to be able to cope with the physical, emotional and social difficulties of life, to become self-motivated and self-directed.

■ Increasing self-esteem in the classroom

Each student in a classroom has a particular level of self-esteem. As in the case of teachers the child's level of self-esteem will largely determine how that child behaves in the classroom. By the time a child arrives into the primary school his home experiences will already have determined how he feels about himself. Parental responses to the child are the looking glass through which the child evaluates himself in terms of his lovability and capability. If he is rarely physically held, is frequently scolded, ridiculed, criticised or compared, is physically abused or has unfair expectations put on him, he will be convinced of his unworthiness. Within the family a child's awareness of his psychological, social and physical characteristics emerges through his family experiences of being loved/not loved and being seen as capable/not capable, clever/ stupid etc. Within the school and classroom a child's evaluation of self emerges through the school and classroom experiences of being popular/unpopular and capable/not capable.

For a teacher to raise students' self-esteem it is necessary that she first elevates her own feelings about self. Research shows that the teacher with high self-esteem produces students with high self-esteem but the converse is also sadly true. It is important for teachers to be aware that every word, facial expression, gesture or action on the part of the teacher gives the student some message about his worth. The teacher needs to ensure that all actions towards students are of a nature that raises self-esteem. This takes considerable awareness and effort but the consequences are highly rewarding in terms of positive school and classroom environments. Elevating students' self-esteem does not take any extra class time. Indeed, it is the students with low self-esteem who take up a great amount of class time. Elevating these students' self-esteem will reduce the class disruption they cause and so make for more teaching time. Also, surely the emotional well-being of the student is as important as his academic development?

The absence of behaviours in the classroom that damage self-esteem is paramount. These include criticism, sarcasm, cynicism, comparison of students, ridicule, scoldings, 'put-down' messages, physical abuse, taunting, negative labelling and ignoring students so that they feel invisible in the classroom. Students, like teachers, have an immense need to be liked, valued and visible. When this does not occur they will subconsciously find ways of being seen, either through withdrawal or aggressive/disruptive behaviours. One of my recommendations to teachers is to ensure that as children file into the classroom and during class time, they make some nonverbal or verbal contact with each of them, thus establishing their visibility within the classroom. The contact can be in the form of eye contact, a greeting, a smile, a nod, a 'welcome back' for a student who was absent, a word of concern for a child who has had, for example, a bereavement in the family or a hospitalised parent, a pat on the shoulder – anything that lets students know that they are positively seen by you. Maintain that type of contact throughout the day.

⤳ Self-esteem-enhancing messages

Apart from the absence of negative behaviours and the presence of contact responses, there are certain powerful messages that teachers can communicate to students that will raise their level of self-esteem. Clearly, the child with low self-esteem needs to experience these messages much more frequently than the middle to high self-esteem student. These messages are:

- Your behaviour is always right.
- You belong.
- You can make sense and order out of your world.
- You are capable in what you do and you please me.
- You are one of a kind and special.
- You have a right to your own unique growing.

➤ Your behaviour is always right.

We have already recognised that maladaptive behaviour is a psychological sign of underlying self-esteem problems, and that it is expedient for the teacher, with the help of the principal and colleagues, to uncover those hidden issues that are causing a student to slide out of mature development and responsibility. It has also been shown that, though the maladaptive behaviours may be saying something 'right' about the student, they can be socially unacceptable to the teacher and other students, and that some constructive responses are needed to curtail the disruption they cause. When students see that a teacher is understanding and compassionate, though positively firm, they are much more likely to respond to the needs of the teacher for responsible behaviours in the classroom. However, if the students feel 'put down' by the teacher, problems are much more likely to escalate.

➤ You belong.

Each student needs to see that he makes a difference, that his presence and absence matter to the teacher and to the school as a whole. The relationship must be such that the student knows without question that he is an important member of the class and school, and is automatically included among 'us' in any formulation of 'us' and 'them'. Belonging is also communicated through photographs and work of students being displayed on classroom walls and school corridors.

➤ You can make sense and order out of your world.

For children security develops from experiencing a world that is generally consistent and predictable in meeting their needs. This is a never-ending process as the needs of children, adolescents and adults keep multiplying. When needs are met only now and again or rarely, the child begins to experience the world (home, classroom, school) as unpredictable and unsafe. He also concludes that it is something within him that has led to his being neglected. On the other hand, when a child's needs are met fairly consistently, the world becomes predictable, or at least understandable, and he concludes that he is basically worthy. The needs of children are many: physical, emotional, intellectual, social, sensual, recreational, spiritual, behavioural, imaginative and creative. Within these need areas they have other needs: the needs to be challenged, to have more and more freedom as they grow older, to be protected, to have limits, to be responsible, to receive advice and counsel, and to experience a sense of humour. Predictability and consistency are the hallmarks of effective classroom management as then children know precisely how the teacher responds to both responsible and irresponsible behaviours. Students also know within this classroom that their needs to be valued, encouraged, recognised and positively corrected will be met consistently.

In this way then the child learns that he can make sense and order of the worlds of classroom and school.

➤ You are capable in what you do and you please me.

Behaviour is the primary means that children use to impress adults and to be competent. It is important to realise that a child's behaviour has two goals: to establish competence in what he does and to develop competence in relationships. Indeed, this ability to elicit expressions of approval and acceptance from parent figures in the child's life will be tested over and over again. Later, this need to impress others extends beyond the immediate family, to teachers, fellow students, relatives and so on. It is not then sufficient for a teacher to notice a child's competency. The teacher must also show obvious approval and acceptance. If that does not happen the child may develop high competence in what he does but he will have no confidence that his behaviour is of any value. Teachers then need to respond at a double level to a student's efforts – recognising the effort and showing they are impressed by it. I deliberately use the term 'effort' as most parents and teachers respond instead to performance, which leads to all sorts of activity and motivational problems for children. Every effort is an attainment and can be shaped up to higher levels of competency. But if an effort is criticised because of performance standard, a child will either stop trying, become tentative about risk-taking (a common phenomenon also among adults!) or overtry. For example, Michael, aged three years, is very proud. He has managed to put on his own shoes for the first time all by himself. 'Look Mommy', he announces, proudly, looking down at his shoes. His mother responds critically, 'you put them on the wrong feet'. She has totally missed what Michael has attained and makes it unlikely he will try again.

Likewise when class or homework is being corrected the emphasis needs to be on the child's effort, and the competence level of that effort is where the child is at. Every teacher with experience knows that you can only work from where the child is at; any 'mistakes' or 'failures' are only indices of the need for persistent effort on the child's part so that his competency will continue to increase. Mistakes and failures are not indicative of capability (which is vast) but only of present levels of knowledge. However, teachers tend to mark academic work on performance rather than on effort.

Let us take a simple example of a child given five spellings to write out and then to present for examination by the teacher. The words and the child's response are as follows:

Word given	Child's response
Boat	Bote
Seat	Seet
Look	Look
Coat	Cote
Rain	Rane

The feedback to the child needs to focus on effort, on where the child is at in terms of competency and on what further efforts are needed to bring about an increase in competency. But what typically happens is the child would get the following feedback:

Word given	Child's response	Typical feedback
Boat	Bote	✗
Seat	Seet	✗
Look	Look	✔
Coat	Cote	✗
Rain	Rain	✗

This can be devastating to a child as it highlights the knowledge he has not got rather than what he has attained. The appropriate feedback is first always give a mark for the effort of doing the spellings and then highlight what has been attained, as follows:

Word given	Child's response	Appropriate feedback
		✔ (for effort)
Boat	Bote	**Bo**te ✔
Seat	Seet	**S**ee**t** ✔ ✔
Look	Look	**Look** ✔
Coat	Cote	**Co**te ✔
Rain	Rane	**Ra**ne ✔

Here the letters that were correctly placed or paired are high-lighted. This reinforces the child for effort and attainment level, and points out to the teacher where the child's next efforts need to be directed – from the starting point of where he is presently at.

The same principles apply when giving feedback to students at university. Highlight what they have attained and give written or verbal suggestions of where their next effort needs to go. It needs to be pointed out strongly that grades are not measures of their capability but only of their present level of knowledge. Let them know that efforts in the directions suggested will reap the reward of more knowledge.

These principles also apply to asking questions of children in the classroom. When a student does not know or only partially knows the answer to your question regarding a particular piece of knowledge, he is ripe for learning. However, if you now pass on to the next student, or even worse still, make some sarcastic remark, you undermine the first student's self-esteem. It is better to help the first student to attain the knowledge level he clearly has not yet reached. In doing that you will not damage your relationship with him and he is more likely to remain motivated to learn. The next question you ask the class must be different from the previous question as otherwise you will be 'showing up' the first student's lack of knowledge.

Another important principle in educating others is to ensure that learning always has only positive associations. Parents need very much to be included in this, as too often home lessons are battlegrounds wherein parents scold, shout, roar, show obvious disapproval or make comparisons. Many teachers still give 'lines' or extra school work as a punishment for misbehaviour and then they wonder why children 'hate' school. The more children experience positive responses to their learning efforts, the more likely it is they will retain their natural curiosity for knowledge and remain highly motivated to learn.

➤ You are one of a kind and special.

The fifth message the child needs to receive from parents and teachers concerns his social self. A person's social self is largely concerned with the sense of being different, separate and unique. No two people are the same. A child's self-esteem requires that he be comfortable with and accepting of his specialness. Most adults do not have that kind of acceptance, the reason being that when they were children their parents and teachers did not celebrate and encourage optimisation of their uniqueness. Difference is not a characteristic that is highly valued in homes and classrooms. A child needs to see clearly that he is accepted and valued for his unique self. Teachers communicate this vital message by letting the child know that there is room in the relationship for him to be different in values, perception, feelings and physical attributes (size, shape, colour). Teachers need also to encourage the child to learn at his own pace. In exercising separation and difference the child needs to know that he does not jeopardise his place in the classroom or school.

> ➤ You have a right to your own unique growing.

This message is concerned with helping children find their own unique life pattern. Teachers and parents who dominate and control prevent the development of this process and so damage self-esteem. The 'mother's vocation' was a reality for many people who went into a religious career in Ireland. This also happens within other professions. I remember helping one young man who had been rejected by his parents (both medical doctors) because he would not do medicine. When he came to see me he had dropped out of college, was feeling really guilty about letting his parents down, and was at a loss as to what he should do about his career development. Many misguided parents want their child to have the opportunities and accomplishments they did not have. The problem is that they forget to ask the child about what he wants. Also times change and, most important of all, the child is not a photocopy of the parent. It would help children enormously if teachers would encourage them to pursue what 'fits' for them and not live other people's lives through responding to parents' and teachers' projections of their own needs. The child who is pursuing his own unique path retains high motivation for learning and the converse is also true. Even if a child acquiesces to parents' or teachers' projections there will always be a hidden resentment and a lack of fulfilment.

↩ Self-esteem-enhancing actions

There are other actions on the part of the teacher that can aid the development of self-esteem in the classroom:

- genuineness and sincerity
- personal time with students
- delegation of routine jobs
- making requests rather than commanding
- positive non-verbal and verbal behaviour.

Being genuine means being a 'real' person and not hiding behind a 'professional mask' or manner. It means being honest, open and spontaneous, and being separate in communicating with students. Staying separate is essential, as a student's behaviour is always a revelation about him and not a message about you as the teacher. If you fail to remain separate you become defensive and conflict between you and the student inevitably ensues. This conflict undermines the child's self-esteem. The teacher who is 'real' also has the ability to recognise success and failure as relative terms and not as absolute measures of children's worth. Being genuine demands that you are honest in your appraisal of yourself and do not project your conflict issues onto students.

The principal issue regarding personal time with students is that the closer your relationship with the student the more it enhances that student's self-esteem. The student with low self-esteem needs far more personal contact than the middle to high self-esteem child. This personal time is not meant to be of an invasive nature but one where interest, concern and affection are shown towards an individual child. All the indicators are that when a student perceives a teacher as liking him, he will not abuse that relationship in any setting, whether within or outside the school.

There are always odd jobs that a teacher needs doing and these provide the opportunity to enhance students' self-esteem. It is best to give these jobs to the pupils with low self-esteem as they are more in need of ways to impress you. Unfortunately teachers tend to give such jobs to the 'more able' students who are not in need of urgent self-esteem enhancement.

When you request you show respect to the student's right to freedom of response and you are egalitarian in communicating. When you command, control and dominate, you lower self-esteem.

Finally, teachers need to guard against non-verbal and verbal communication that is detrimental to self-esteem development. As has been pointed out, children are quite sensitive to non-verbal cues from others, cues that can communicate messages along the dimensions of likes–dislikes, interested–not interested and superior–inferior. Examples are body posture, eye contact, body orientation, tone of voice, pauses in speech, speed of speech, facial expression and gestures. Verbal messages are more obvious and it can be seen more clearly how they can enhance or reduce self-esteem. Again, it is essential that they are of a positive nature such as encouraging, affirming, praising, valuing and calming. Be sure that your verbal message is congruent with your non-verbal communication. If there is incongruence, if there is a discrepancy between the two levels, the child will nearly always relate to the non-verbal message.

❑ *Key insights*

- Students' maladaptive behaviours are indicators of 'hidden' conflict issues unique to each child.
- Students' maladaptive behaviours are signs which should not be allowed to be shown in vain.
- A student's problematic behaviour is called 'maladaptive' because it never resolves the hidden conflict issue.
- It is not difficult for teachers to identify the at-risk student.
- Students' maladaptive responses can be usefully categorised as undercontrol and overcontrol behaviours.
- A student who avoids, is overinvolved in or is hostile to academic effort and demands is masking a self-esteem problem.
- Some maladaptive behaviours, though psychologically 'right', are socially unacceptable.

- A student's self-esteem in the classroom is largely determined by the type of teacher–student relationship operating in that classroom.
- The only relationship that enhances students' self-esteem is an empathic, unconditional one.
- There is a high correlation between level of self-esteem, motivation to learn and academic attainment.
- Students with middle to low self-esteem may use avoidance or compensation to avoid the humiliation of failure.
- Constructive and realistic challenges are needed for children to develop a sense of capability.
- Without attention to self-esteem students with learning difficulties are unlikely to make long-term progress.
- All actions of the teacher towards the student communicate a message about the child's worth and this happens whether the teacher is aware or not of this process.
- Every academic effort is an attainment.
- Mistakes and failures are opportunities for learning.
- Comparison of one student with another is an act of rejection of the student compared and it also puts pressure on the 'model' student to be always 'one up'.
- Learning must always have only positive associations.
- Attendance to students' self-esteem will lead to greater academic effort.

❑ *Key actions*

- Discover the hidden conflicts of students manifesting either undercontrol or overcontrol maladaptive behaviours in your classroom.
- Seek early identification of the at-risk student to prevent escalation of maladaptive behaviours.
- Be aware of creating a destructive type of relationship with students in the classroom.
- Create an empathic and unconditional relationship with each student in the classroom.
- Do not break a relationship with a student because of a maladaptive behaviour on his part.

- Positively and firmly correct the maladaptive behaviour but not the person of the student.
- Put the emphasis on responding to academic effort rather than academic performance.
- Be sure there is not too wide a gap between your academic expectations and a student's present level of attainment.
- Employ mistakes and failures as opportunities for teaching not criticising.
- Avoid the use of criticism, ridiculing, scolding, 'put-down' messages, sarcasm and cynicism.
- Find ways to make each student visible in your classroom.
- Send verbal and non-verbal messages that elevate students' self-esteem.
- Make it clear to students that both their presence and absence matter.
- Be predictable and consistent in the way you respond to students.
- Correct students' work in a way that emphasises effort and present level of attainment, and indicate where the next academic effort needs to be directed.
- Do not ask another student the same question that you have asked of a student who did not know the answer.
- Spend personal time with each student.
- Pay particular attention to the student with low self-esteem by means of personal time, delegation of routine jobs and frequent affirmation.

CHAPTER 5

The Classroom

❏ *Classroom control is not the teacher's responsibility*

It is not the teacher's job to control students in the classroom! This goes contrary to what I learned and practised as a teacher. However, closer examination of traditional discipline practices reveals that it is a recipe for conflict to get one person to control another. You know that as an adult when a person attempts to control you or gives unsolicited advice you react defensively. The same holds for children and adolescents. Effective classroom management is based on the principle that each member of the class, student and teacher, is responsible for his own self-control. It is not then the job of the teacher to control students but the responsibility of students to control themselves. Equally the teacher has the responsibility to be in control of himself and any loss of control with students is an abrogation of that responsibility. Indeed, if a teacher frequently loses control he is hardly in a position to request students to take charge of themselves. Furthermore, this teacher models lack of self-control for students and it is the tendency of children to imitate adults. Yet another issue is that the teacher who responds negatively and aggressively to students is, in fact, giving them control over him. In this classroom the students know they can 'get under the skin' of the teacher and, as students generally are not given a lot of power in classrooms, this bit of power becomes a weapon to be used, particularly when their self-esteem is under threat.

Good classroom management is aimed at educating students to take responsibility for themselves. In any social system the members have certain responsibilities so that order, safety, fairness, justice and harmony are promoted. For example, there are certain responsibilities drivers have so that road systems are effectively utilised. When you are caught for speeding in a thirty-miles per hour zone, or for illegal parking, blaming the policeman or traffic warden is hardly fair as you are the one who chose to act irresponsibly. The sanctions are there to ensure responsibility; you chose the risk of sanction when you acted irresponsibly. Most people are very pleased with the strong sanctions that are now in vogue for drunken driving. The person who loses his driving licence due to that irresponsibility has chosen that sanction; it is only a further act of irresponsibility to blame the policeman for the imposed sanction.

A school and a classroom are social systems. Within these systems the responsibility for particular functions must be clearly spelt out. There are different responsibilities for the different members of the systems: the principal, the vice-principal, teachers with A or B posts, teachers with responsibilities for particular groups of children, the class teacher, the students, the secretaries and others involved. The particular responsibilities of students within and outside the classroom need to be typed out and pinned up in every classroom. This list of student responsibilities needs also to clearly specify what sanctions there are when a student fails to meet the agreed responsibility. At the start of the school year and the beginning of every term, the teacher needs to remind the students of those responsibilities and their accompanying sanctions. Most of all he must point out that the choice lies with them, not with the teacher. He then gives the students the opportunity to voice any objections to the outlined responsibilities, and conveys those to the committee responsible for drawing up these responsibilities. (These issues are dealt with in more detail below; see pp. 113–18.)

It is wise for teachers to remember that students need frequent reminding of their responsibilities. Also, one of the responsibilities of teachers (like that of a traffic warden) is to ensure that children do not slide out of responsibility. In order to do so, a teacher needs to have an unconditional valuing of each student and an awareness of the unique potential of each student. When a student chooses to be irresponsible, the teacher justly and fairly imposes the agreed and outlined sanction that the student chose to risk when she acted irresponsibly. It is important that the sanction fits the crime as unjust consequences rarely induce responsible behaviour.

Classroom management is largely then the responsibility of students. The teacher's responsibility is to ensure that the devised school and classroom systems are effectively implemented. Frequent reviewing of the effectiveness of any social system is desirable. In this approach the teacher is not seen as a disciplinarian but rather as a presenter of choices and their consequences (both positive and sanctions), and the students are put in clear responsibility of themselves. Giving responsibility to students and believing in their ability to meet it are powerful boosts to their self-esteem.

❑ *Causes of children's difficulties*

Control difficulties within classrooms have become a major source of stress for teachers. Old authoritarian methods rarely work anymore and some teachers are left floundering as to how to respond to behavioural problems within the classroom.

You have seen that these behavioural difficulties are signs of underlying emotional or social difficulties of children and that attention to these hidden conflicts is essential if long-term progress is to be achieved. Nevertheless, some direct positive response to the behavioural disruption is needed in the short term as learning best takes place in an environment of relative calm and harmony. Most teachers are aware that the student who persistently disrupts the class often has a difficult home background, and very often back-up and co-operation from the parents of this student is difficult to acquire. Nonetheless, some knowledge of the possible causes of the student's emotional and behavioural difficulties makes for a better understanding of the problematic behaviour and for a more wide-ranging constructive response to the display of such difficulties.

Emotional and behavioural difficulties in children can arise as a consequence of two types of circumstances, which can often coincide. Firstly, the problems may spring from short-comings in the process of socialisation to which all children are normally exposed. Examples of these are:

- the lack of a continuous relationship with mother or mother-substitute or just one adult during the first three years of life
- later poor modelling by parents, who do not respect themselves or each other, of maladaptive behaviours such as aggression, non-assertiveness, poor communication skills, irresponsibility
- absence of essential experiences, for example when a child is reared in a subculture (travelling community, area of high unemployment) whose values, morals and standards of behaviour differ from those of the larger culture into which the child may have to fit as she grows up.

The second set of circumstances that may lead to emotional and behavioural problems in children is where the child is exposed to excessive pressure from outside or inside herself. External pressures are the more common and come from, for example, dominating, controlling, hypercritical parenting, alcoholism of one or both parents, marital discord, domestic violence, lack of social ability in either parent or hostility arising from a three-generation family living under the same roof. Difficulties can also arise from 'spoiling' children as these children do not learn self-control or the ability to tolerate delayed gratification. Inconsistency of positive parenting skills also puts pressure on children as these children do not know where the limits are and they can often play one parent off against another: like adults, they will slide out of responsibilities if they get the chance. Pressures arising from within children include physical or mental handicap, developmental delays and poor knowledge levels when they enter school. At least one-third of children who have physical or mental handicaps also develop emotional difficulties.

It is also a fact that not all children's problems are a product of their home situations. Some problems can be directly traced to the classroom or school situations. The most common of these problems is fear of the teacher. Generally speaking, teachers of whom children are fearful have a repertoire of behaviours that are of a destructive nature, perhaps the most common being sarcasm, cynicism, irritability, impatience, intolerance and verbal aggressiveness. Sarcasm, cynicism and verbal aggressiveness are unfair weapons that a teacher uses against students whose respect he cannot obtain. They precipitate either worse behaviour or withdrawal and silent resentment on the part of the targeted students, and they are always emotionally disruptive. The students who are passive get hurt, those who are verbally quick 'talk back', and those who are hostile make scenes. The result is a disruptive classroom environment where no one gets much learning done.

Fear of examinations is another problem that arises all too commonly nowadays within the classroom setting. Its effects are well known: anxiety, concentration problems, memory difficulties, insomnia, headaches, muscle tension, 'mental blocks', depression, suicidal feelings and so on. This fear comes from too great a pressure for marks by parents or teachers or both. Teachers should seek to make academic tests interesting and challenging to students of different levels of ability. They need to ease the pressure on students and encourage them to do the best they can. Most of all they need to remind students that scholastic performance is not an index of their worth as persons.

Finally, some students, particularly in early adolescence, have a fear of standing up and speaking in class. This may stem from, for example, sensitivity over their height or voice change; teachers need to be sensitive to this difficulty and attempt to make classwork as informal as possible.

❏ *Undercontrol problems in classrooms*

Earlier a distinction was made between problems of under-control and overcontrol and it was indicated that it is the former difficulties that primarily affect classroom management (see pp. 77–81). The main undercontrol problems that make it difficult for teachers to conduct their classes are listed below. This is by no means an exhaustive list.

Student's undercontrol behaviours within classrooms	
Start of class	
• Enters room noisily • Pushes and shoves other students • Shouts out to others • Bangs desk on sitting down	• Does not have materials needed for class • Avoids eye contact • Ignores teacher's requests
During class	
• Tries to be funny • Turns around in class • Talks in class • Rocks in chair • Walks around classroom • Talks and mutters to self • Distracts others • Lifts desk with knees • Starts singing • Makes distracting verbal or physical noises • Constantly fidgets with apparatus	• Reacts aggressively to feedback • Does not answer questions addressed to her • Ignores requests for responsibility on her part • Throws paper missiles around class • Interferes with other students' work • Fails to hand up homework • Teases and taunts other students ➥

• Ignores teacher's requests • Has temper outbursts • Steals other children's possessions • Absconds from classroom	• Refuses to do classwork • Makes irrelevant comments • Damages other students' property

End of class

• Rushes out of class • Pushes and shoves others • Shouts loudly • Makes 'smart alec' remarks	• Avoids eye contact • Ignores teacher's requests for orderly exit • Ignores teacher's requests to stay behind

Outside of class

• Bullies other students • Breaks rule of no smoking • Defaces walls • Damages school property	• Steals other people's belongings • Races along school corridors • Shouts in school corridors

A student who is regularly showing any of these difficulties needs an immediate, consistent and predictable response. These behavioural manifestations are additional to any learning difficulties she may have and they make this student stand out from her peers. Knowing that such a student has a difficult family situation or a different cultural background is helpful but it is not a reason to say 'nothing can be done'. All the evidence suggests that a child with emotional and behavioural difficulties or cultural differences will adapt to an environment where she is valued, affirmed, respected and positively shaped into accepting responsibility within the classroom and school.

❑ *Maladaptive behaviours of teachers within classrooms*

Given that some problems can be traced to factors within the school, it is wise for teachers and principals to look to their own behaviours and see whether these may be a trigger to students' disruptive responses. A list of such behaviours is given below. These maladaptive behaviours on the part of the teacher are indicators of underlying insecurity issues that he needs to own and take responsibility to change.

Teachers' inappropriate behaviours within the classroom

Teacher–student communication

- Shout at students
- Order, dominate and control students
- Employ cynicism and sarcasm as means of control
- Ridicule, scold and criticise students
- Label students as 'stupid', 'dull', 'weak', 'lazy', etc.
- Physically threaten students
- Push and shove students
- Are violent towards students
- Give school work or 'lines' as punishments
- Do not listen to students
- Compare one student with another
- Are judgmental
- Do not like some students
- Have obvious favourites
- Do not know students' first names
- Do not call students by their first names
- Are too strict
- Are impatient with students who are slow in understanding a lesson
- Expect too much of students
- Do not care whether students work or not
- Do not feel any affection for students
- Punish mistakes and failures
- Do not help when the work is difficult
- Never apologise for mistakes
- Do not say 'please' and 'thank you' to students
- Are inconsistent and unpredictable in response to troublesome behaviour

Teachers' attitudes to lessons

- Waste time
- Do not make lessons interesting
- Are not prepared for lessons
- Leave class half-way through a lesson
- Pass on to next lesson without regard to students who have not mastered first lesson
- Are programme-centred rather than student-centred

Teachers' own emotional state

- Frequently irritable and moody
- Hate teaching
- Doubt own teaching competence
- Fear loss of classroom control
- Worry how colleagues view them
- Want students to like them
- Have low self-esteem
- Fear students

❏ *Essential aspects of classroom management*

Below is a checklist of in-class teacher behaviours that I regard as vital for effective classroom management. Practice of these attitudes and behaviours will lead to a decrease in classroom difficulties and act as a means of preventing other problems developing.

Checklist of positive in-class teacher behaviours
1. Has an unconditional relationship with each student
2. Recognises the influence of self-esteem on learning
3. Sees person and behaviour as separate issues
4. Knows that learning is not an index of capability
5. Views success and failure as relative terms
6. Employs mistakes and failures as opportunities for learning
7. Puts emphasis on effort rather than performance
8. Makes sure that learning has only positive associations
9. Does not project own needs onto students
10. Sees a student's problem behaviour as saying something about that student, not about the teacher
11. Stays calm and relaxed at all times
12. Is fair, consistent and predictable in responses to all students
13. Frequently praises and affirms students
14. Is positively firm in the face of difficult behaviour from students
15. Listens to all sides
16. Prepares lessons well
17. Requests rather than commands
18. Is child-centred rather than programme-centred
19. Is not trapped into conflict with student presenting maladaptive behaviour
20. Knows when help is needed

It can be seen that most of these pointers have already been discussed in previous chapters which focused on self-esteem issues. This just confirms that attention to the self-esteem of both teacher and student is central to classroom management. A few of the behaviours need further elaboration.

A surprising revelation for me was that learning is not an index of a person's capability (item 4)! Conditioning had led me to believe that genetics rather than environment was the determinant of intellectual functioning. However, research has now shown that the best predictor of intellectual functioning is socio-economic status. Only about 1 or 2 per cent of children from 'lower class' families go on to third-level education compared to over 20 per cent for 'middle-class' families. It is hardly the case that the former have less capability than the latter. The difference is in opportunities. Middle-class children come from homes where sensory stimulation is qualitatively and quantitatively high, one-to-one verbal encounters are frequent, education is highly valued, children are encouraged to talk, read and play constructively, parents themselves are often still pursuing further education and children are more motivated to learn. The level of knowledge and motivation to learn of these children is far greater by the time they come to primary school and puts them at a distinct advantage over children who come from 'disadvantaged' situations. Unfortunately, the child's level of scholastic response often becomes the determinant of academic labelling on a range from highly intelligent to mentally handicapped. Labels in turn determine teachers' expectations of children and indeed children's expectations of themselves: when a child self-labels (internalisation of labels from significant adults), she tends to live up or down to that label. For example, children who believe they are poor readers read poorly. Adults also label themselves in terms of intellectual activities. Most adults believe they are useless at public speaking or voicing questions in a group, and they generally fulfil their own prophecies. Many adults believe they are no good at mathematics and dread any public exposure to mathematical questions. However, I have no doubt that each person has the capacity to comprehend any branch of knowledge given belief in self, application and appropriate learning opportunities. What a boost to a child's self-esteem is the communication: 'you are immensely capable and your present level of knowledge is no index of your capabilities as a person'. Knowledge is peculiar to cultures not to intelligence. For example, the Aborigine people, whilst having extremely poor verbal functioning compared to people in Western society, have highly developed and advanced right-brain functioning in terms of visual, spatial and mechanical abilities. It is important therefore that teachers do not confuse knowledge with capability. Teaching is about increasing children's knowledge; you cannot increase a child's intellectual capacity.

Item 14 recommends that you be positively firm in the face of a child's undercontrol behaviour. This also links up with item 19, which advises not to get into conflict with a student who is out of control. The issue here is that aggression breeds aggression and that negative responding on a teacher's part to a student's maladaptive actions will only escalate the situation. Indeed, if possible, the best strategy is to give no attention to the student, as often the subconscious ploy is to gain attention. The no-attention response often defuses the student's under-controlled reactions. If a response has to be shown it is essential that you stay calm and in self-control, and firmly but positively request the student to desist from the unacceptable behaviour. There is little chance of this happening if you lose control of yourself. Furthermore, your loss of control gives the student control over you and further licence to engage in her disruptive responses. Sometimes no matter what you do the student may persist in the maladaptive behaviours. Possible strategies in such a situation are discussed below (see pp. 118–22).

Listening to all sides is a crucial requirement in teaching (item 15). Listening is the first and, indeed, most important act in communication. Children need to be both heard and seen. For example, frequent enquiries of students regarding any difficulties they might be having with your subject will often prevent future accusations of unfairness or of not understanding sections of the course. It certainly will communicate your concern for them and your willingness to listen to their side. In conflict situations be wary of judging too quickly; listen to all sides before making a final assessment of what has transpired.

❑ *Designing a student responsibility system*

Traditional discipline systems tended to stress the 'do nots' demanded within schools and classrooms. Such an approach does not tell students what they should do and hence does not foster their self-control and responsibility. The word 'discipline' has negative associations for many of us who came through traditional school systems and I much prefer to use the phrase 'educating for responsibility'.

■ Student responsibilities

In designing a system of responsibility within and outside the classroom, a list of the key responsibilities of students needs to be drawn up by a committee which has management, principal, vice-principal, teacher, student and parent representatives. It is best that such a list be kept to a minimum.

Examples of students' responsibilities at school

In-class responsibilities

- Is on time for class
- Walks in an orderly way into class
- Sits in seat immediately
- Stays in seat
- Moves around classroom in orderly way
- Waits quietly for instructions and directions
- Hands up assigned homework
- Communicates in respectful fashion to teachers and fellow students
- Respects other people's property
- Speaks at an acceptable noise level
- Responds positively to requests from teachers
- When disturbed or angry requests personal time with teacher
- When class teacher does not respond to reasonable complaints of unjust behaviour, brings issues to committee for student responsibility

Out-of-class responsibilities

- Walks along corridors in orderly fashion
- Respects school and other people's property
- Speaks at an acceptable noise level
- Plays in school yard in a way that is safe for others
- Communicates in respectful way to others

Students need to be frequently reminded of these responsibilities. Indeed a copy of them and the accompanying sanctions for irresponsibility should be posted in every classroom and sent to the parents of each child. An explanation or rationale for these responsibilities, perhaps typed below the list of responsibilities, also needs to be given. Guidelines for such explanations are:

- Relative quiet needed for learning to occur
- Safety of self and others
- Taking care of one's own and others' belongings
- Making the best effort
- Creation of positive teacher–student and student–student relationships

■ Positive use of sanctions

Any social system has to employ sanctions in order to ensure adherence to agreed responsibilities. Within a school, it is essential that sanctions be employed within a context where teachers have unconditional positive relationships with students, use positive teacher–student communication, emphasise academic effort rather than performance and clearly and consistently reinforce effort. Sanctions must be implemented in such a way that the student knows precisely how she has been irresponsible and what exactly is required of her the next time. Sanctions must educate for responsibility; they must not be a means of 'putting down' children. The positive use of sanctions has certain clear characteristics:

1. When possible, the sanction used should be *the natural result of the irresponsible behaviour*. For example, if a student wastes time in class, a natural sanction is to deprive her of break or leisure time. If a student in temper throws materials all over the classroom, a natural sanction is to get her to tidy up the room.

2. Sanctions must be *predictable and consistent*. This means that students always know where responsibility lies and know that breaching that line will always lead to the application of a sanction. Furthermore, students need to know

that no matter which teacher is involved or which student chooses to be irresponsible the same sanction will occur.

3. Sanctions must always be *fair and just*: the sanction must always fit the irresponsibility. When sanctions are agreed by a committee and not left up to the whim of a particular teacher, the possibility of injustice is considerably lessened. Frequent reviews of the responsibility system also guard against injustice.

4. Sanctions must be *impersonal*. The teacher who loses his temper with a student who is inattentive and assigns a sanction that arises from the teacher's own projections or needs for attention will not be effective with students. The students know that the sanction is only an outlet for the teacher's dependency and they blame him rather than themselves.

5. Sanctions must *emphasise what is expected* of students so that they become an opportunity for more responsible behaviour and self-control.

6. Sanctions should be *withheld* until the teacher understands the psychological 'rightness' of the maladaptive behaviour and assigns the sanction in a way that clearly demonstrates that understanding.

7. Sanctions must be *positively and calmly applied* so that the student does not become fearful of the teacher. Fear blocks the communication path between student and teacher. Furthermore, a student who is frightened may agree to anything, but when she recovers, she will have learned nothing and her next act of irresponsibility may be worse than the first.

8. Sanctions must *never involve the assignment of 'lines' or extra homework*. Learning must only have positive associations for students.

9. The *student's first name* must always be used in assigning a sanction.

What sanctions are available for use within a school system? Different social systems demand different solutions and each school needs to determine the best responsibility system for its unique culture. Therefore this list is just a general guideline.

Sanctions available for schools

- Positive and firm request for responsible behaviour
- Withdrawing attention from irresponsible action (this very often is effective, as the ploy can be to get a teacher's attention)
- Deprivation of privileges (the possible loss of an activity that a student thoroughly enjoys becomes a strong motivation for responsibility)
- Detention with a meaningful purpose: this needs to be supervised and the supervisor needs clear directions on what academic task has been assigned to the student; this task could be, for example, completion of class and homework not done but not extra 'punishment' assignments
- Non-academic duties during break times, e.g. collecting litter
- Warnings of being sent to class teacher (peculiar to second-level schools), vice-principal or principal
- Placement in a lower class (most students hate this because their irresponsibility becomes public knowledge to a younger peer group they might want to impress)
- Being on report (many schools now employ a report-card system which teachers are required to mark at the end of each class)
- Being sent to class teacher, vice-principal or principal
- Letter to parents
- Meeting with parents (it is advisable that both parents be invited in to discuss their child's progress in school)
- Written warning of suspension given to student and sent to parents
- Suspension
- Expulsion; this is a last resort where the needs of the teachers and other students outweigh those of the student who is recalcitrant or who needs more specialised education or psychological or social help

---

❑ *Implementing a student responsibility system*

The effective implementation of an agreed system of responsibility depends on the full cooperation of all teachers with strong back-up from principals, vice-principals, management boards and parents. Within the school predictability and consistency across all teachers for all students and within each setting are paramount. Any breach of these conditions weakens the system and allows students to play off one teacher against another or one situation against another. The context of close relationships with students, belief in students' capability, and emphasis on and frequent reinforcement of academic effort must be maintained at all times. Such a school environment not only prevents the development of many problems but makes it easier to correct irresponsibility when it does occur.

There will be better commitment to a system if all parties are included in the design of the system. The formation of a committee who are responsible for monitoring and reviewing the system is important. Again such a committee is best comprised of representatives from the various groups: teachers, students (except in the case of very young children), parents and management. The decisions of this committee must not be overruled by any one teacher or principal. Otherwise the power of the committee and of the system of responsibility will be weakened. One of the major functions of the committee is to arbitrate on the 'grey' areas of what a particular responsibility or sanction precisely means. Different responsibilities and sanctions may mean different things to different students and teachers. When a student or teacher needs clarification on an issue, redress to the committee should be made. Its decision must be final.

❑ *Responding to a student who is recalcitrant*

Even after a teacher has developed a positive classroom atmosphere through close relationships with students, has made lessons as interesting and student-centred as possible, is relaxed and calm in teaching, allows students to constructively voice their needs, grievances or worries, and has led students to a reasonable level of self-control, he may find himself faced with a student showing undercontrol behaviours. The behaviours that most distress teachers are aggressive outbursts or insulting verbal behaviour from students. The tendency is to react negatively to these, but unfortunately such a response only escalates the student's problematic actions.

It is wise to be aware that aggressiveness or insolence on a student's part inevitably arises from the hidden need to be loved, valued and accepted, and is preceded by some experience during which the student felt hurt, angry or frightened. When the student has 'cooled down' the teacher should give the student a normal amount of affection and safety, and then attempt to discover what hurt, angered or frightened her. Even though some sanction may still need to be imposed it can be done now within the context of this understanding. Indeed, the teacher may find that he needs to change some aspect of his behaviour towards the student.

Nevertheless, when a student exhibits out-of-control behaviour some immediate action is needed in order to diffuse the situation. Sometimes the best action is no action. Verbally confronting an out-of-control student rarely works (even though the teacher may do it in a positive but firm way) as the student is highly emotionally upset and requests for reasonable behaviour are likely to fall on deaf ears. There is nothing better than hurt, anger or fear to deafen a student to the voice of reason. Emotion in this context is always stronger than cognition. The no-action response to the student and the encouragement of the rest of the class to continue the given academic activity take the focus off the distressed student. Behaviour always has the function of eliciting a response and so it can quickly extinguish when no reaction is forthcoming. If this happens then no reference to the student's maladaptive behaviour must be made during the remainder of the class. However, at the end of the class, it is important that the teacher takes some private and personal time with the student so that they can jointly discover what led to the problematic behaviour. This may require requesting a colleague to cover the next class for a short period of time.

When a student's behaviour puts the teacher or other students at risk then some decisive action is required. If other students are at risk the teacher needs to quietly and calmly request the class to leave the classroom and assemble in an orderly way in a designated place. One of the more responsible students should be requested to relay what is happening to the principal and to ask the principal to take responsibility for the class in the meantime. Do not physically approach the student but stay at a distance, silent and calm.

When a student physically attacks a teacher it is essential that the teacher does not retaliate as this would only aggravate the situation. He should calmly back away from the student, maintaining strong eye contact (so that the student sees that the teacher is in control), request the class to leave, and send a student for immediate back-up from the nearest teacher.

No matter what the situation is, analysis of the event must take place afterwards in a secure setting for both student and teacher. A useful way to analyse maladaptive behaviour is by means of the ABC system.

■ ABC analysis of maladaptive behaviour

- *A stands for antecedent*: what went on before the onset of the problematic behaviour, whether between the teacher and student or student and peer, or some event prior to coming into class or school. Other possible antecedents may be covert such as aggressive thought patterns or 'bottled-up' resentments. Very often it is these external or internal events that trigger the student's maladaptive behaviours. When these are isolated a clearer picture is revealed. For example the teacher may discover that it was his negative language that offended the student or the student may discover that it was her own 'nursing' of unresolved hurts that led to the outburst. In either case something can be corrected so that these triggers are removed from social interactions. Sometimes it may be some aspect of the classroom setting that acts as a trigger, for example an overhot room, being seated next to a student who bullies or teases, or inadequate equipment for assigned project.

- *B stands for behaviour*: what precisely the student has done. It could be the use of foul language, refusal to carry out an assignment or inattentiveness in class. The more clearly the behaviour is defined, the easier it is to define the responsibility that the student will be expected to take on as part of the resolution of the conflict. In the examples given above, the clear responsibilities are appropriate communication of needs, acceptance of class assignments and application to classwork.

• *C stands for consequence*: what follows the behaviour. For example, very often students' academic efforts, politeness or caring for property go unnoticed, leading to extinction of such responsible behaviours. Reinforcement of responsible behaviours is not frequent enough within most homes and classrooms. There are different types of reinforcers – social, tangible, token – and when these are given contingent on efforts to be responsible they lead to an increase in such behaviours. Social reinforcers (praise, pat on the back, affirmation, encouragement, smile) are the most powerful of all. Token reinforcers include points, credits, stars and money, all of which can be exchanged for tangible reinforcers such as sweets, toys, books, trip to cinema or an excursion to town. You have seen that when the consequence of a student's aggression is aggression, this serves only to increase the student's maladaptive behaviour, whereas if the consequence is no attention at all to the aggressive behaviour, this often leads to an extinction or reduction of that behaviour.

By examining the three phases of a sequence of behaviour much can be learned about what needs to be changed at both the antecedent and consequence stages in order to bring about a change at the behavioural level. The ABC analysis is certainly helpful in the immediate situation but it does not address the deeper affective issues of why one student reacts more aggressively or hypersensitively than another student. Such issues may only emerge on acquiring a deeper insight into the student's internal and external life (see Chapter 4).

When a student persists in engaging in irresponsible behaviour, in spite of teachers' and others' best efforts to help the student, then some outside intervention is required. Clearly, if the child has a learning difficulty then some special teaching for learning difficulties may be the option needed. A note of caution here is that many children's poor intellectual functioning arises from deeper affective problems and when these are resolved children begin to thrive academically. Therefore, any assessment of a child needs to be holistic so that all aspects of her life are examined. For example, a problematic child may come from a subculture where the values, morals, attitudes and standards of behaviour are very different to that of the school. The attempt to impose the 'majority' culture on this child may result in the child feeling out of place in spite of her best efforts and may lead her to act out these conflicts. A school more suited to her subculture would be more appropriate for this student. Moreover, there is a certain disrespect in imposing one's own culture on another person of a different culture. Other students exhibiting persistent difficulties may require individual counselling or psychotherapy but preferably family therapy. When parents become involved in the resolution of their child's conflicts speedy progress can be made. It is important to recall here that sometimes it is the teacher who requires psychological help.

Early detection and intervention for students displaying socially unacceptable behaviour within the school and classroom are essential. Too often problems are allowed run too long before positive and decisive action is taken. Other students and teachers should not have to tolerate disruption in classes over a long period of time. Control difficulties have become a major cause of burn-out in teachers and resolution of these issues must become a priority for each school, with the back-up of psychological and social services as well as support and resource allocation from the Department of Education.

❑ *Use of back-up professional services*

It is clear that many of the problems of students are either emotional or social in origin and that these students and their families require help from psychological and social agencies. Traditionally there has been an intellectual and learning assessment psychological service available to schools but this has been too narrow in its focus to be able to resolve students' emotional and social difficulties. Furthermore, there are teachers who need psychotherapeutic help and such a service needs to be made available in a highly confidential context. Many schools have no back-up help services and teachers are left floundering as to what to do with children in distress. A confrontative style of management (see pp. 138–9) is needed to demand the development and availability of these services: teachers are not psychologists or social workers or family therapists. Many career guidance teachers, whose role has been greatly pared down because of financial cutbacks, are loaded with trying to help such children. Again, this is not their brief and neither has their professional training equipped them to deal with such children. Some career guidance teachers, to their credit and at their own expense, have done various counselling, psychotherapy or family therapy courses. Whilst this is laudable it does mean that there is less onus on the Department of Education in providing in-school student counselling services. There is certainly some movement towards providing more comprehensive back-up services to schools. Indeed, it is in the interests of the Departments of Education and Health to provide such services, as early detection and intervention will mean that children in distress will not later become clients of adolescent and adult psychological and social services.

Deciding whether a student's difficulties require specialised attention is not necessarily as easy as might be assumed. Emotional and social signs of disturbance are, by and large, exaggerations, deficits and debilitating combinations of behaviour patterns common to all children. The following are the main factors to consider before deciding whether the problems of a student need professional intervention.

- Age and stage of the child's development

Whether or not many problems are considered in need of professional help will depend on the student's age. Behaviours which are common and normal at some ages are maladaptive at others. For example, temper tantrums are common in pre-school children and hence 'the terrible twos'. Bedwetting occurs frequently in children up to the age of three or four years but it is clearly maladaptive in a child of over five years and even more alarming in an adolescent. Younger children have many fears because they are still becoming acquainted with aspects of their world. However, school-going children and adolescents manifesting fears of the dark, of failure, of conflict or of other students are clearly manifesting hidden emotional or social conflicts.

■ Frequency of behaviour

The more frequently a behavioural difficulty is occurring, the more likely it is that specialised attention is needed. An odd occurrence may only indicate a transient difficulty which clears up with the passage of time and life experience.

■ Intensity of behaviour

The more extreme the emotional intensity (extreme anger, panic, timidity) or the avoidance or aggressive behavioural patterns, the higher the indicators are that this student (or teacher!) needs help. For example, about one-third of children show reluctance in going to school, but a child who has developed a phobia of school will exhibit severe distress and panic feelings when attempts are made to bring her to school. Excessive distress will manifest itself in the child's physiological state (increased heart rate, paling, vomiting, stomach pains, trembling, etc.), in verbally expressed feelings of fear and discomfort, and in attempts to avoid or escape from school.

■ Persistence of behaviour

The longer behaviours such as aggression, tantrums, noncooperation, fears, phobias, timidity, bedwetting, soiling, withdrawal, depression or sadness persist, the greater the indicators are that the student needs help. Many adolescents who display persistent difficulties are carrying problems from childhood which, regrettably, were not picked up at that stage of development. Secondary difficulties will also have developed for these adolescents, as scholastically and socially they will have fallen far behind their peers – yet another blow to their self-esteem.

- Student's home environment

It has been my experience in working with some students that it is their parents who need help and not them. Very often I do little to treat the children but put great emphasis on changing the parents' relationship with the child. Many parents project their own insecurities, unmet needs, perfectionism, rigidities, anxieties, pessimism and helplessness onto their children, and unless these problems are resolved the children of these parents will continue to be at risk. The maladaptive behaviour of children can be a normal response to an abnormal situation. The abnormality resides in the environment rather than in the child. For example, aggressive responses in a student may be the consequences of modelling or imitating parental behaviour. Alternatively, the student's aggression may be a function of the blocking of her needs within a rigid, restrictive, dominating and controlling family code of behaviour. Furthermore, problems of theft, delinquency and truancy in adolescents have been associated with parental attitudes of indifference. In these circumstances the child, finding no security in the home, will often seek acceptance from her peer group and follow the norms of that group. Within the group, activities such as truancy, theft and aggression might be normal — yet another example of the influence of the environment rather than pathology within the young person.

- Student's school and classroom environments

Not all problems of children arise from their family circumstances: a school environment or a particular teacher's behaviour may explain why a child is experiencing some emotional and behavioural difficulties. You have already seen how a child from a subculture may not 'fit in' to a school environment with a very different culture. This child needs a more appropriate school environment to meet her particular needs. There are teachers who have their own deep emotional difficulties; these may manifest themselves through either aggression, controlling, dominating, cynicism and sarcasm or timidity, fearfulness and anxiety within the classroom, leading to difficulties for students. Here it is the teachers who need professional help and not the student. Many school principals have difficulty in approaching these teachers and some confidential system is needed that principals could employ in such situations. Sometimes it is the school principal who is problematic and it is important that teaching staff have some means of relaying concerns and worries to an effective source.

Most students who are referred for specialised help are reacting with maladaptive behaviour to traumatic home or school experiences in the present or past. As such, the pre-ferred help should be psychotherapy or family therapy. Drug treatment is not to be recommended. The past thirty years have seen the emergence of a variety of helping methods: behaviour therapy, cognitive therapy, gestalt psychotherapy, client-centred psychotherapy. These approaches either attempt to change the environment a child lives in or deal directly with the child's emotional and behavioural difficulties. Family ther-apy involves treating the whole family and identifying some dysfunction within the system that is the source of a child's difficulties. These treatments are often effective and the high demands for them are indicative of that effectiveness. Finally, it is my conviction that an understanding of the student's inner life, and of that of her parents and teachers, must always precede the choice of therapeutic approach.

❏ *Key insights*

- Classroom control is the responsibility of students.
- It is a recipe for conflict to get one person to control another.
- A teacher has the responsibility to retain control of himself.
- When a teacher loses control of self he gives the students control over him.
- Classroom management is about educating children to take responsibility for themselves.
- Giving responsibility to students and believing in their ability to meet it are powerful boosts to their self-esteem.
- Persistent emotional and behavioural difficulties of students arise from either deficiencies in the process of socialisation or excessive pressure inside or outside the child.

- It is problems of undercontrol that mostly disrupt learning within classrooms.
- Knowing that a student who is problematic has a difficult home situation is no justification for saying 'nothing can be done'.
- Students with emotional and behavioural difficulties respond positively to a school and classroom environment where they are consistently loved, valued, affirmed, encouraged and praised.
- Students' problems can arise from factors within the school and classroom.
- Positive in-class teacher behaviours promote a healthy classroom environment.
- Knowledge is not an index of intelligence.
- Aggression breeds aggression.
- Listening is the first act of communication.
- A system of student responsibility within and outside the classroom should be devised by representatives of all parties involved.
- A rationale for student responsibilities needs to be provided.
- Sanctions must educate for responsibility.
- Predictability and consistency are the hallmarks of an effective system of responsibility.
- The decision of a committee for student responsibility must not be overruled by any one teacher or school principal.
- Aggression or insolence on a student's part arises from a hidden need to be loved, valued and accepted and is preceded by some experience during which the student felt hurt, angry or frightened.
- Hurt, anger and fear deafen students to the voice of reason.
- An ABC analysis of a distressing incident reveals immediate remedial actions that can be taken.
- When problems persist, in spite of the best efforts of teachers and others, outside professional help is needed.
- Early detection and intervention for students displaying maladaptive behaviours is important for the student, other students, the teachers and the school.

- Back-up psychological and social services are needed for students and teachers displaying persistent problematic behaviours.
- Preferred treatments are psychotherapy and family therapy.

❏ **Key actions**

- Stay calm, relaxed and in control of self at all times.
- Frequently remind students of their classroom responsibilities and the sanctions for irresponsible behaviours.
- Let students know that the choice of being responsible or irresponsible lies with them and it is they who choose an assigned sanction.
- Avoid the use of inappropriate behaviours that damage students' self-esteem.
- Arrange professional help for your own emotional difficulties.
- Avoid getting into conflict with a student who is exhibiting undercontrol difficulties.
- Listen to all sides.
- Display list of student responsibilities within each classroom.
- Apply sanctions in a way that demonstrates understanding of the underlying difficulties of students.
- Be predictable and consistent in your responses to students' maladaptive behaviours across all students and all situations.
- Remember that sometimes the best action is no action.
- Jointly explore with a student what underlies that student's disruptive actions.
- When needed, ask for support and help from colleagues.

The School

❑ *The effective school*

All the indicators are that an effective school has characteristic patterns of behaviour revolving around three main themes: high expectations of students and staff, emotional responsiveness and effective leadership. The first two themes involve interactions that lead to the elevation of self-esteem of both students and teachers.

▪ High expectations

The high expectations exhibit a belief in students' and teachers' immense capacity to learn and to cope with all aspects of life.

The emphasis is on effort, not performance, and students and teachers are frequently affirmed and encouraged in their academic, social, behavioural and emotional efforts. Mistakes and failures are seen as opportunities for further development. Children are not compared to each other academically as each child is seen as a unique human being possessing his own special way of perceiving and interacting with the world. Teaching is child-centred and works from a child's present level of attainment. All efforts are seen as attainments and feedback on scholastic work is given in such a way that the student knows precisely where his next academic efforts need to be focused. Teachers themselves are encouraged to affirm their own uniqueness and efforts. They too employ mistakes and failures as stepping stones to further academic knowledge and understanding of human behaviour. There is a sharing of knowledge and experience among teachers, and requests for help in teaching a particular subject are actively encouraged. Children are also encouraged to seek help when needed. Learning and study have only positive associations.

■ Emotional responsiveness

Emotional responsiveness is concerned with the creation of unconditional valuing relationships between teacher and teacher, teacher and student, principal and staff, student and student, and teachers and parents. The uniqueness of each person within the school system is emphasised and respected. Affirmation, warmth, praise, encouragement, support and comfort are frequent features of the interrelationships between all members of the system. The development of close relationships and support networks are key issues. There is an absence of any behaviour that damages the self-esteem of anyone within the system such as destructive criticism, comparisons of one person with another, ridiculing, scolding, cynicism and sarcasm. At the same time, any behaviour that is disrespectful of anyone within the system is firmly responded to and appropriately agreed sanctions are assigned. Open, relating communication is taught and practised, beginning with the principal and teachers who act as models for the students.

Feelings are seen as barometers of the present emotional state of a person and emergency feelings are seen as indicators of conflicts that need resolution. Responsibility for self is clearly laid on the shoulders of each teacher and student, and any attempt to slide out of responsibility is firmly confronted. At all times a clear distinction is made between person and behaviour. When maladaptive behaviours (whether of students or teachers) are confronted, the focus is on behaviour, and the maintenance of the relationship is seen as essential for the resolution of the conflict issue. Listening is seen as essential.

A school environment that provides such emotional responsiveness, responsible permissiveness, support, understanding, compassion, unconditionality and positive firmness leads to the elevation of each person's self-esteem. This, in turn, brings about further emotional maturity on the part of each person and an expanding cycle of physical, psychological and social wellness develops. The involvement of parents is seen as essential: they are actively encouraged to back up the school system and to create a similar environment in the home.

■ Effective leadership

The third characteristic of the effective school is effective leadership. Mature leadership is a crucial issue within any system. When parents have low or middle self-esteem, they will have many deficits in emotional maturity, communication, problem-solving, expression of feelings, independence and closeness, and so inevitably the family system suffers. So too with other organisations. The insecure, low to middle self-esteem leader inevitably undermines the self-esteem of those below her in the organisation, leading to a dysfunctional system.

↩ Main characteristics

The most important characteristic of an effective school principal is high self-esteem. Such a leader will have:

- Value and belief in self and life
- Ability to unconditionally value others
- A capacity for focused attention

- Ability to appraise teachers' and students' efforts
- Problem-solving and conflict-resolution skills

⮑ Style of leadership

The style of leadership will entail:

- Assertiveness with regard to own beliefs and conflict issues
- Affirmation of staff and students
- Flexibility in the face of difference
- Internal control and independence
- Challenging of self, staff and students
- Tolerance of mistakes, failures and vulnerability
- Responsiveness to all expressed feelings by staff and students
- High expectation of staff and students in terms of academic, social and emotional efforts
- Availability
- Approachability
- Listening skills
- Decisiveness
- Direct and clear communication
- Provision of safety and security for distressed staff or students
- Confidentiality
- Non-conformity

⮑ Role model

The effective leader also acts as a role model for others in the system in terms of:

- Awareness of own strengths and weaknesses
- Disclosure of own need for help and support
- Balanced lifestyle
- Close personal relationships and support systems
- Flexibility and openness to other people's differences
- Responsibility for own professional, emotional and social needs
- Hope and meaning in all aspects of life

- Direct and clear communication
- Physical fitness
- Healthy diet
- Relaxation and calmness
- Effective time-management

⇔ Time-management

Many school principals find themselves overburdened with a wide variety of demands and more effective time-management could ease that situation for them.

Checklist for effective time-management
• Have a daily time-management system
• Account for each hour of your work time
• Make lists of tasks to be done
• Identify priorities
• Have short, medium and long-term goals
• Realistically estimate time allocation for tasks
• Programme only 60 per cent of your time
• Book yourself some free time
• Allow for 'travelling time' between tasks
• Adhere to your timetable
• Allocate time for making phone calls
• Use answering machine when busy
• Finish each task before going on to the next
• Revise your time-scheduling regularly

Principals who have self-esteem difficulties will find it difficult to carry out these suggestions as they tend to be dependent on others for approval and engage in behaviours that block effective time-management.

Blocks to effective time-management
• Have difficulty in saying 'no' to demands made on you • Give too much time to particular staff member or student • Avoid doing things that you do not like doing • Avoid issues that threaten your self-esteem • Avoid confrontation on difficult issues • Take long breaks • Usually arrive late • Often do useless tasks • Frequently need someone else to check your work • Lack office equipment needed to do a job • Meet people socially during work time • Have difficulty in concentrating for long periods

⮑ Delegation

Many school principals have difficulties in delegating work. The following questions can help to identify the areas of work that can be delegated. Make a list under each question:

- As principal what work are you required to do?
- What do staff members have to do?
- As principal what are you doing now that others could take over?
- As principal what are you doing now that colleagues might do more effectively?

Be sure you appreciate the workload your colleagues have before delegating further work. Most importantly, do not be afraid to ask for help and support. Effective delegation rests on your knowing full well the responsibilities each of your staff carry and assigning tasks to the person who is best fitted for them. Be sure you clearly define the task you are delegating and the level of responsibility and time allocation involved. Be available for consultation.

Blocks to delegation	
• You want to get all the credit.	This is a sure sign of insecurity and dependency.
• You know best what has to be done.	This is a 'superior' attitude arising from low self-esteem and blocks others from showing their effectiveness.
• You want things done perfectly.	This shows fear of failure and mistakes, communicates distrust to colleagues and blocks risk-taking.
• Staff should see you need help.	You are responsible for your own needs; staff are not mind-readers; and it is your responsibility as manager to delegate tasks.
• Staff may not want to take on assigned tasks.	Delegation of tasks is a joint activity, initiated by the school principal but the ultimate decision as to who does what should come from the staff group.
• You want to be liked.	This mirrors dependency and low self-esteem. Ironically you will gain far more respect in being direct and clear in communication and being just and consistent. You are unlikely to be accepted if you become the 'martyr' who carries all responsibilities and never asks for help.

↪ Relating to staff

Many of the issues on the development of positive staff relationships and staff morale were covered in Chapter 3: open and relating communication patterns, staff affirmation, group decision-making, availability, approachability, understanding the nature of a staff member's rigidity and responding effectively to it. A further issue is to check how you relate to colleagues. Good social skills, effective active listening and assertiveness are essential aspects of positively relating to staff. The questions listed below will help you to evaluate how well you as a principal relate to your staff.

How do you relate to your staff?

- Do you call staff members by their first names?
- Do you greet staff members when you meet them?
- Are you approachable?
- Are you available?
- Do colleagues communicate to you personal, interpersonal and professional difficulties?
- Do you ask for feedback on your management style from staff?
- Do you have an effective management style?
- Do you express your emergency feelings when appropriate?
- Do you respond compassionately to a teacher in stress?
- Do you negotiate work responsibilities with staff?
- Are you predictable and consistent?
- Are you aware and accepting of your strengths and weaknesses?
- Do you frequently affirm and encourage colleagues?
- Are decisions made jointly by you and the staff?
- Do you confront teachers who are engaging in socially unacceptable behaviours within the classroom or staffroom?
- Do you confront rather than avoid difficult issues?
- Are you independent of staff's opinion of you?
- Do you make difficult decisions when you have to?

❏ *Coping strategies within schools*

There are many aspects of the educational system and of particular school and classroom systems that are dysfunctional leading to students feeling anxious, hurt, angry or rebellious; teachers feeling pressurised, fearful, aggressive or burnt out; and principals and vice-principals feeling overburdened with multiple responsibilities, trying to motivate a demoralised staff and lacking basic back-up services such as secretarial and maintenance assistants. Many principals and teachers adapt to dysfunctional systems, saying 'you have to work within the system' – even if it is causing many problems for individuals.

There are basically two ways teachers can react to dysfunctional systems:

- conforming coping
- confrontative coping.

■ Conforming coping

The conforming coping style is illustrated in Figure 1. Most teachers accept that there are many features both in the theory and practice of education that need to change. The extent of those changes will vary from school to school and, for example, what works for so-called advantaged schools may not be applicable to many so-called disadvantaged schools. The general tendency is to conform to the system in place, roll up one's sleeves and do one's best. This style of coping often gains admiration and praise for teachers from parents and government bodies which serves to reinforce that coping style. It also means that the Department of Education is given more power to formulate policies without too much interference from schools. Furthermore, this style of coping does not measure the effects this system has on staff and students. They are seen as casualties of the system. The system then is greater than the individuals within it. But a system that results in stress, absenteeism, low morale, low self-esteem, burn-out and psychosomatic illnesses in staff members, and anxiety, maladaptive behaviours, absenteeism, low self-esteem and school drop-out in students must be dysfunctional and should not be tolerated. However, the more staff resort to conforming strategies and adapt to dysfunctional circumstances, the greater the likelihood of the continuation of problems within the school system.

Figure 1: Conforming coping style

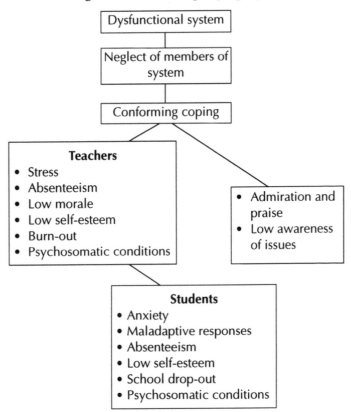

■ Confrontative coping

Confrontative coping (see Figure 2) means that the person does not lie down under issues that need addressing, does not accept that members of the system should become stressed and burnt out, and strives for support and for solutions from both within and outside the school system. Most of all this coping style is person-centred rather than system-centred. When a system fails to meet the needs of individuals within it, the person questions the suitability of the system and does not blame or condemn the distressed individual (whether principal, teacher or pupil). The person coping in this way will attempt to change aspects of the system or campaign among outside bodies for the setting up of an alternative system to meet the needs of the troubled individuals. Such a style of coping means that individuals within the system feel listened to and cared for, and that attempts will always be made to meet their reasonable needs either within or outside the system. The consequence is more highly motivated staff and students who will have higher self-esteem, better physical health, high attendance and positive attitudes to learning. The morale of the school will be higher. Furthermore, such a staff will gain the respect and admiration of others, and parents and officials within the Department of Education will have a greater awareness of the changes that are needed within education.

Figure 2: Confrontative coping style

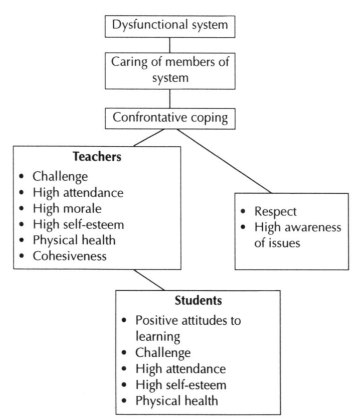

❏ *Whole-school approach*

▪ Shared responsibility

Many of the issues involved in a whole-school approach have already arisen in earlier parts of this book. The principle underlying a whole-school approach is that of shared responsibility, whereby every member of the school system is involved in the development of a school environment where each person is respected, valued, affirmed, secure and safe. Staff cohesiveness is essential to the development and maintenance of such a supportive system. No longer can teachers be left isolated in their classrooms to cope with the depth and range of emotional and behavioural problems of some students. Teachers need the back-up of the principal and colleagues.

▪ Predictability and consistency

Predictability and consistency across all teachers are vital for the agreed standards of behaviour to be reinforced and for breaches of that behaviour to be dealt with firmly and fairly. Teachers need very clear guidelines on how to respond to problematic behaviour within classrooms and school grounds. If individual teachers operate their own classroom management systems then the likelihood of abuses of the overall system is greater.

▪ Effective communication

Certainly a whole-school approach depends on effective leadership and effective communication patterns. Briefly, what is needed here is a clear and well-communicated management system that ensures that each member of staff knows who does what, who is responsible for each area of the school and where the lines of accountability are. Students also need to know who to go to for what, who is in charge of a particular area and what responsibilities they have within the school system.

▪ Staff support and development

A whole-school approach also recognises the need for staff support systems and staff development not only in terms of academic knowledge and teaching techniques, but also a greater awareness of human behaviour within schools, homes and society in general. This has been a major area of neglect in teacher training. There are signs that the need for the continuing education of teachers is being recognised and that the provision of in-service courses, suitable to the culture and needs of particular schools, is beginning. There is also growing awareness of the stress and burn-out within the teaching profession and of the need for a more caring environment within schools in order to help those individuals. Confidential counselling services are needed for highly distressed teachers. However such services must not become an excuse for doing nothing within the school system. An individual teacher may derive a lot of benefit from psychotherapy, but if she has to return to a non-supportive school environment, it is unlikely that the personal gains made will be maintained.

■ School identity

Finally, the identity of a school is an important aspect of a whole-school approach. The stronger, more dynamic and unique a school's identity, the greater the loyalty and commitment of teachers and students. They will feel proud to be members of such a unique system. The creation, maintenance and further development of such an identity is the responsibility of all members of this system. There is a whole range of issues in the creation of a school's identity:

- Clear and dynamic goals
- Visible and creative display of school name at entrance gate and hall
- Attractive and well-maintained school grounds
- Attractive interior decor
- Good maintenance of interior and exterior environment
- School games and interschool competitions
- Display on corridor walls of teacher and student attainments
- Class photographs on walls
- Regular social functions

- Parent–teacher committees
- Evening courses for different community groups
- School plays, musicals and concerts
- Past pupils' organisation
- Past teachers' organisation
- School involvement in caring for socially disadvantaged
- School involvement in caring for environment
- Educational research
- School newsletter or magazine
- Teachers' publications

❏ *Involvement of parents*

Many teachers have felt threatened by the increasing involvement of parents in education. Indeed, some teachers hate and dread teacher–parent meetings and see them as something to be got through rather than a source of help and support. Parents themselves also feel threatened by such meetings as they fear that teachers may say critical things about their children and they often blame themselves for their children's problems. Sometimes they will blame teachers; this will cause defensiveness on the teacher's part, and reduce the likelihood of a clear analysis and resolution of the problem behaviour. The involvement of parents whose children are presenting difficulties within the classroom is necessary if any long-term resolution is to be achieved. The earlier the consultation with parents the better. As has already been said many times, children who are highly problematic come from problematic homes. Much can be done within the school to compensate for shortcomings within the home, but the cooperation of parents leads to a speedier change in children's behaviour. It is the same in therapy: when parents accept the need for family therapy, attend as needed, and develop awareness and more effective coping and relating strategies, a wellness cycle is created within the family.

Approaching parents about the difficulties of their children demands a high degree of sensitivity to their vulnerability. Inevitably, the parents of pupils presenting with problems within the school will themselves have self-esteem problems, will be dependent and will possibly be highly defensive through aggression, manipulation or passivity. It is important that these parents do not feel in any way blamed or judged. Parents do not deliberately neglect, harm or put undue pressure on their children; the process is quite subconscious. Change will only occur through gently helping them to become aware of how what happens in the home has a damaging effect on their child. It is important too that parents feel valued and liked by the teacher, and that the teacher affirms them for many of the positive aspects of the home setting. The teacher's approach to the parents needs to be one of concern for the mature development in all areas of functioning of their child. The parents need to hear the teacher as valuing and caring for the child and requesting their help to increase the child's coping within the school. They must not perceive the teacher as blaming, judging or labelling their child. Through regular meetings a joint approach may be developed to aid the child. Regular reviews and openness to informal consultation by phone, letter or quick 'drop in' should be made available to both parties. When some outside agency needs to be employed, this must be done in a highly confidential way.

However, the involvement of parents needs to be wider than just problem-solving. Parents can do much to create positive and challenging attitudes to education in the home. They can give children a love of learning. By the time children come to primary school their attitudes to learning may already have been formed. If the home was not qualitatively stimulating, if parents did not engage in one-to-one talking with children, if they did not frequently read stories for their children and if they punished mistakes and failures, then it is unlikely the newcomer to school will have retained his natural curiosity for learning. Courses for parents as educators need to be established within both primary and secondary schools. Parents are not experts in how best to provide for the intellectual development of their children: teachers can provide them with that expertise. Other courses on the emotional and social development of children or the sexual development of children or the behavioural management of children or coping with adolescents could also be offered within the school setting. Conflict-resolution skills, problem-solving skills, effective communication skills, stress-management skills and assertiveness skills could also be taught to parents. Many teachers could also benefit from participation in these courses. Indeed, their attendance with parents would create stronger ties with parents. A parents' committee could be formed to organise many of these events.

Circularising parents on developments within the school will add to their inclusion in school matters. Parent representatives should be on all major committees within the school system. Parents could also be encouraged to contribute to the school newsletter or magazine. Some parents may be available to offer assistance with activities inside and outside the school – a much underused resource. The crucial point is that parents have talents, skills, knowledge and expertise that can add considerably to the effectiveness of a school system.

❑ *Key insights*

- High expectations, emotional responsiveness and effective leadership are the main characteristics of an effective school.
- High self-esteem is the hallmark of an effective principal.
- Time-management and delegation of work are central issues for effective leadership.
- Good social skills, active listening and assertiveness are essential aspects of positive relating to staff.
- Conforming coping style is neglectful of all members of a school system.
- Confrontative coping style means the person confronts the issues that need addressing.
- Shared responsibility is the basic principle underlying a whole-school approach.
- Staff development and staff support systems have been major areas of neglect in schools and teacher training.
- A confidential counselling service for principals and teachers who are in distress needs to be developed.
- Schools can be the centre for many community activities.

- The involvement of parents whose children are problematic within the school is essential for long-term resolution of difficulties.
- Approaching parents about the difficulties of their children demands a high degree of sensitivity to their vulnerability.
- Parents can do much to create positive and challenging attitudes to education in the home.
- Teachers can provide parents with the expertise on how best to provide for the intellectual development of children in the home.
- Parents have talents, skills, knowledge and expertise that can add considerably to the effectiveness of a school.

❑ *Key actions*

- Principals to be positive role models for teachers and students.
- Principals to devise an effective time-management system and identify blocks to its implementation.
- Principals to check attitudes to delegation of work.
- Principals to evaluate how well they relate to staff.
- Staff to develop a climate of shared responsibility coupled with consistency and predictability of responses to students' problematic behaviour across all staff members.
- All to take responsibility to create a clear and well-communicated management system which will aid the development of an effective whole-school approach.
- All to take responsibility for the development of a supportive and safe staff environment.
- Determine the steps needed for a unique school identity.
- Establish close liaison with parents.
- Set up courses within the school for parents as educators.
- Involve parents as assistants for activities in and out of school.

Albert, Linda, *A Teacher's Guide to Co-Operative Discipline*, Minnesota: American Guidance Service, 1989

Briggs, Dorothy Corkille, *Your Child's Self-Esteem*, Garden City, New York: Doubleday, 1967

Canfield, Jack and Wells, Harold C., *100 Ways to Enhance Self-Control in the Classroom*, Englewood Cliffs, New Jersey: Prentice Hall, 1976

Charlesworth, Edward A. and Nathan, Ronald G., *Stress Management, A Comprehensive Guide to Your Well-being*, Corgi Books, 1987

Dobson, Fitzgerald, *How to Discipline with Love*, New York: Rawson Associates, 1977

Gray, Harry and Freeman, Andrea, *Teaching Without Stress*, London: Paul Chapman Publishing, 1987

Glaser, William, *Schools Without Failure*, New York: Harper and Row, 1969

Jarnpolsky, Gerald G., *Teach Only Love*, New York: Bantam, 1983

Lawrence, Denis, *Enhancing Self-Esteem in the Classroom*, London: Paul Chapman Publishing, 1987

Mason, L. John, *Guide to Stress Reduction*, Los Angeles: Peace Press, 1980

O'Connor, Joyce and Ruddle, Helen, *Cherished Equally?*, Limerick: Social Research Centre, NIHE. Copies of this book may be obtained from the Mid-Western Health Board, 31–33 Catherine Street, Limerick.

Peck, M. Scott, *The Road Less Travelled*, Century Paperback Series, 1987

Satir, Virginia, *Conjoint Family Therapy*, London: Souvenir Press, 1980

Satir, Virginia, *Peoplemaking*, Palo Alto, California: Science and Behaviour Books, 1972

Stone, Lyndsey, *Managing Difficult Children in School*, Oxford: Basic Blackwell, 1990